Kathy,
Wishing you a future filled with sunshine, laughter, and smiles.
God Bless,
Jerry Stecker

Who Will Care for You in Your Time of Need . . . Formulating a Smart Family Plan to Age-in-Place

Who Will Care for You in Your Time of Need...

Formulating a Smart Family Plan to Age-in-Place

John Hemphill

Copyright © 2016 by John Hemphill.

Library of Congress Control Number:		2016912606
ISBN:	Hardcover	978-1-5245-3024-2
	Softcover	978-1-5245-3025-9
	eBook	978-1-5245-3026-6

All rights reserved. No part of this book may be reproduced or transmitted in any form or by any means, electronic or mechanical, including photocopying, recording, or by any information storage and retrieval system, without permission in writing from the copyright owner.

Any people depicted in stock imagery provided by Thinkstock are models, and such images are being used for illustrative purposes only.
Certain stock imagery © Thinkstock.

Print information available on the last page.

Rev. date: 12/06/2016

To order additional copies of this book, contact:
Xlibris
1-888-795-4274
www.Xlibris.com
Orders@Xlibris.com
699466

Contents

SECTION I
THE RECKONING! 1

Chapter 1   Who Will Care for You . . .
                 When Health, Memory, and Ability
                 to Live Independently Are Questioned? 3
Chapter 2   Do You Have an
                 Aging-in-Place Smart Family Plan? 8
Chapter 3   The Crossroad Challenge 16

SECTION II
THE CONUNDRUM! 25

Chapter 4   Expanding the Family Household 27
Chapter 5   The Reckoning Crisis by the Numbers 36
Chapter 6   Sandwich Generations Engulfed
                 in a Lifestyle of Family Caregiving 44

SECTION III
THE AWAKENING 53

Chapter 7   Who Will Care for You . . .
                 When Your Children Can't or Won't 55
Chapter 8   Health Mechanisms Contributing
                 to People Who Will Need Caregiving 72
Chapter 9   Understanding the Necessity
                 for Formulating an Early, Smart
                 Family Plan to Age-in-Place 83

SECTION IV
THE INTERVENTION (PART I) **91**

Chapter 10 Module Component #1
            Understanding the Synergistic
            Effects of Chronic Disease
            Conditions on Health and Aging 93
Chapter 11 Module Component #2
            Physical Activity and Exercise
            to Stay Healthy and Independent 106
Chapter 12 Module Component #3
            Eating Healthy to Live Healthy 117
Chapter 13 Module Component #4
            Environmental Home-Modification
            Health and Safety Strategies
            for Staying in Your Home! 134

SECTION V
THE INTERVENTION (PART II) **151**

Chapter 14 Module Component #5
            In-Home, Long-Term Care Planning 153
Chapter 15 Module Component #6
            Legal and Life-Care Planning 169
Chapter 16 Module Component #7
            Family Dynamics of Caregiving 188

Special Notice 211
About The Author 213
Acknowledgment 215

The Reckoning

Who Will Care for You in Your Time of Need!

Whether you're nearing retirement or have decades before you enter retirement, you will be confronted with four inevitable lifestyle crises: (1) How will you manage your own care when your independence is in question? (2) Will you have the resources and assistance to help manage your care? (3) Will you have one or more chronic health conditions/disabilities that will jeopardize your future independence? (4) In addition to your care, will you be responsible for the care of an aging parent, family relative, or friend?

This book aims to direct people of all ages to start thinking early about their future lives by developing and formulating a smart family plan to live healthy to stay in their own homes (aging in place). The goal is simple: formulate early a smart aging-in-place plan for a future lifestyle of health, senior independence, and safeguarded quality of life.

John Hemphill

Section I
The Reckoning!

"There are only four kinds of people in this world: Those who have been caregivers; those who currently are caregivers; those who will be caregivers; and those who will need caregivers"

Former First Lady Rosalynn Carter

Chapter 1

Who Will Care for You . . . When Health, Memory, and Ability to Live Independently Are Questioned?

The Reckoning Crisis—Do You Have an Aging-in-Place Plan?

Chances are, if you have picked up this book, at least one of three things has happened: one you are currently an unpaid caregiver for a family member or friend; two you are contemplating the roles, duties, and responsibilities of an unpaid family caregiver; or three, you have not come to reckon with a real-life fact that you may be in need of a caregiver in your distant future.

Let's take a quick journey to unveil this *reckoning crisis* looming before us: who will care for you when health, memory, and physical abilities to live independently are questioned? The answer may surprise you, but people need to seriously consider two key factors in these modern days: *(1) start living healthy now and (2) assess your caregiving needs to gracefully age in place.*

First, looming before you in this modern-day era is a premonition that most of you will need caregivers when failing health and memory jeopardize your ability to stay in your own homes. Secondly your quality of life will most likely become compromised due to a health illness or disability. Finally, your long-term, *in-home family*- caregiving needs may not come from an immediate family member!

Pushing this reckoning crisis are sandwich generations (baby boomers and young adults) caring for elderly parents/grandparents and children. These generations have given no consideration for planning their long-term care future or formulating an early smart family plan to age-in-place. Why is this important?

Simply put, someday in the near future is a question to contemplate, who will care for you if family members are unable to attend to your needs? The question baby boomers and younger generations need to consider lies in the understanding and meaning of aging in place.

> Aging in place is a movement that supports the idea that most people should be allowed to live out their lives in their own homes rather than being forced into assisted living or nursing homes. And the Centers for Disease Control (CDC) define *aging-in-place* as the ability to live in one's own home and community safely, independently, and comfortably, regardless of age, income, or ability level.

The goal for adult generations, as this reckoning crisis comes to fruition, is to start early, formulating a smart family plan to age in place. A smart family plan is your healthy-living goals to maintain and improve your quality of life for living longer, better in order to stay healthy and independent upon approaching your senior years.

A good smart family plan focus is maintaining a lifelong quality of life. It should cover you and your spouse, or significant other, health and wellness goals for staying healthy, home-safety modifications, long-term care finances, caregiving/caregiver plans, and other key components that will be outlined later in this book.

Looking ahead at this looming crisis for living healthy and caregiving needs are other sociopolitical and economic in-place challenges that can be forecast for the future:

1) The anticipated growth of baby boomers turning sixty-five over the next two decades will put a tremendous strain on families, their quality of life, and housing accommodations to live safely.
2) The roles of government (federal and state) to help support older adult programs and services have been severely cut over the past decade.
3) Huge labor shortages for both skilled medical professionals and in-home aides and attendants may not be available to serve this fast-growing, aging population.
4) High cost of long-term senior-care facilities will continue to skyrocket, and senior housing inventory will not meet the increased demand. (Example: the 2016 median cost for a Florida Assisted Living Facility is $3,045/month and for a Home Health Aide is $3,766/month. Availability will be limited, and cost will continue to increase.)
5) What chronic illness, chronic disease condition, or disability will compromise the quality of life and independence to stay in your home?

I have personally experienced this reckoning crisis, which I'm referring to as our modern-day healthy-living tsunami. It's very clear that our quality of life for maintaining one's health, mind, and independence will be tied to our ability for staying healthy. Therefore, staying healthy and living healthy must be—and should be—an early, lifelong practice to age gracefully (aging-in-place).

Staying healthy to age-in-place is only one part of the quality-of-life equation. One must also consider who will care for you when the mind, health, and independence jeopardize your safety.

Let me take the time to illustrate my family-caregiving observation and the reason for writing this book. While caring for my wife's parents living with us, I tumbled upon one important revelation:

> Caring for parents may have a negative effect on our children observing our caregiving duties and struggles.

That's why the question statement "Who will care for you?" is important. I will never forget my oldest daughter's comment one day when observing how my wife and I cared for her parents living with us for ten years. Looking back on our elder-care lifestyle, it was often difficult to go out to dinner or go on family vacations without extensive planning and caregiving expenses.

One particular evening while just trying to make a simple plan to go out for dinner, my daughter observed us making precautionary caregiving arrangements to ensure her parents' comfort and safety made a profound statement. She said empathetically in a not-so-kidding manner:

> "I'm not going through all this trouble for you guys when you get old. I'm just going to find a good retirement home to put you guys in."

Wow! That comment got our attention, and we began to ask ourselves that question, "Who will care for us in our time of need?" The day of reckoning is here for all to start considering *we will all need caregivers* someday when health, memories, and independence erode us. The question remains, "Who will be there for you?"

I hope this book, in some way, will be your quality-of-life and aging-in-place lifestyle lesson guide. The sole purpose and intent for writing this book is to educate people of all ages to start learning early about **the seven core lifestyle principles for making a smart family plan to age-in-place**.

Life will go on. And for many of you, life's unexpected medical circumstances will quickly change with time. The question still remains, "Will you be prepared?" Looking back on my professional public health experience and personal family-caregiving experiences, I have seen the elder care and aging-in-place reckoning crisis forecast.

Are you ready to take ownership of your lifestyle to make living healthy to age in place a top priority? Time waits for no one; however, living a longer and healthier life is a practice that can be obtained.

This book will give you insights to this crisis looming ahead. My experiences have taught me one important lesson for living healthy to age in place: start formulating early your own smart family plan to age in place, for in the words of actor Wilford Brimley, "It's the right thing to do!"

CHAPTER 2

Do You Have an Aging-in-Place Smart Family Plan?

Aging-in-Place Planning Questions and My Family Story

Let's begin to assess your family-lifestyle plans for aging in place. The goal of this simple exercise is to bring attention to aging questions that will help you develop your plan. The plan is intended to bring awareness to your quality-of-life issues that will help you and your spouse maintain your dignity, safety, and independence to gracefully age in the comfort of your own home and familiar surroundings (*aging in place*).

Review the following questions below. They are intended to help you think about developing your smart family plan to age-in-place. As you proceed to answer these questions, let me remind you to ponder on several caregiving and family-lifestyle challenges: (1) your family-caregiving needs may not come from an immediate family member, and (2) lifestyle challenges for living healthy and sustaining good wellness and practice habits will reap great rewards as you get older.

Aging-in-place planning questions to consider are:

- Who will provide your future family-caregiving needs?
- Do you have a sibling(s) who has the temperament to serve as an unpaid family caregiver?
- Does your sibling(s) have family issues and live far away or in another state?
- Are you without children? Then who will care for you?
- What burden will your spouse contend with having a partner with a severe health illness or cognitive disability?
- Do you have substantial personal resources and financial savings to handle the family-caregiving crisis if a loved one has a disability?
- Based on projected baby boomer trends, will there be long-term care facilities to handle the demand in your area?
- Do you have a home that is suitable to age in place?
- Have you made any *in-home*, long-term care plans/ arrangements or inquiries?

You may not know the answers to these questions listed above. However, I suggest you review the questions carefully, for sections IV and V, there are seven core aging-in-place lifestyle lesson modules that will help you get a complete handle on the reckoning crisis looming ahead in these modern days. These lesson modules are your key core components for formulating your smart family plan to age in place.

My Family Story (Parts 1 and 2)—Sandwiched Caring for Parents and Children

My family life experience as an unpaid family caregiver began some thirty-seven years ago in the mid-1970s. My dad, a World War II service veteran, separated and, living in the suburb outside Philadelphia, Pennsylvania, suffered a massive stroke. My dad, at age fifty-six, had a stroke that left him partially incapacitated with only eighty-five percent movement on his left side. He successfully rehabbed himself, regaining most mobility functions, but he eventually, had to use the assistance of a walking cane to get around the rest of his life.

I attended to my dad's needs only as a distant caregiver assistant. Newly employed and married for four years, I could only give emotional support and some physical help with household repairs when I was in town. My sister's family (living across the state in Pittsburgh) and my aunt (living in Philadelphia) provided the brunt of caregiving oversight and service.

My dad, maintained a daily military lifestyle regimen for twenty years after his stroke. He being a proud and independent person, made it easy caring for him from a distance. He attended to his own activities for daily living doing his own household laundry, cleaning, other activities and home repairs. He would also religiously take his early-morning mile walk, usually around the mall in the neighborhood, and frequently assisted the staff at the local VFW Lodge.

My sister and aunt took on the majority of caregiving duties as care managers. My sister, living four hours away, would make daily morning phone calls to assess Dad's health and state of mind each day. Later on in life, she took over his finances, paying his bills. My aunt, living thirty minutes away from my dad, would check on him three to four times during the week.

My aunt would visit him to monitor his health, mental stability, and household upkeep functions. She would also monitor and parcel out his medications by day in weekly pill containers. My aunt and a local high school friend, also a VA veteran, would take turns taking him to various medical appointments and grocery shopping.

Life during the final three years of his life, was not at all difficult. My dad recognized that his memory was failing knew that it was dangerous for him to live alone.

One particular incident my dad spoke candidly about was a nearly fatal fall-injury incidence on the stairwell of the cellar basement. He miraculously missed falling on a hand truck at the bottom of his stairwell. Life was amazingly good to him surviving that and other falls with no serious injuries or broken bones. Maybe his daily physical-activity regimen kept him from a serious injury.

Later, another ministroke left him hospitalized again. He was then transferred to a local rehab facility for rehabilitation. Realizing living alone was no longer an option, the rehab facility consultant advised my sister and aunt to relocate him in an independent living facility about five minutes away from my aunt's home.

Living at the nursing home facility for a year and a half, we noticed that my dad's health and spirits began to diminish. My dad's lifestyle consisted of two simple habits: exercising, walking around the local mall in the wee morning hours-- and being a handyman--always fixing or doing something.

This was quite a difficult challenge for him to not have his independence to do things. Even exercising at the senior center met resistance. He was not allowed to walk in the wee morning hours in the facility hallways, stairways, and campus grounds where it was forbidden. When he could no longer do those simple things because the facility safety policy, his lifestyle quickly deteriorated.

Later while in the facility, he started experiencing frequent lower abdominal pain. The bouts started to recur quite frequently and with much pain. Finally, my dad could not fight the good fight any longer and told my sister to let him go, saying, "I've lived my life."

My sister, believing there was a medical screw-up at the facility that exacerbated his condition, did not pursue the incident any further. He finally passed away in 2009, my sister and aunt keeping his wish. The family focused attention to caring for our mother, eighty-six, with Parkinson's disease, living in New Jersey.

The Jones (In-Law) Family Story—Part 2

Life as a distant family caregiver took another turn in the late 1990s when my wife's parents, living in southern New Jersey, were showing early signs that we now know were dementia. Pat, my wife and a registered nurse, is the youngest of five siblings (three brothers and one other sister).

Pat and her sister-in-law were the responsible family caregivers for her parents. The two provided the brunt of elder care assistance for her dad, a World War II vet and Tuskegee Airmen, eighty-one years of age, and her mother, a homemaker, age eighty.

Family life for Pat as the principal distant caregiver was challenging. My professional job had transferred me to Atlanta, Georgia in 2000, so family life was strictly on her to maintain. My oldest daughter was attending college on the West Coast, and the youngest daughter was just entering her senior year in high school.

My wife maintained the household in Delaware and cared for her parents by making frequent trips to New Jersey. She was still working full-time and attended frequent high school functions for our daughter. She also had to make all the necessary arrangements with a realtor company to have the house placed on the market to sell.

Pat's weekends, for a year and half, consisted of traveling sixty minutes from Delaware to New Jersey to attend to her parents. Both her parents had serious medical issues. Her dad's medical history included: high blood pressure, diabetes (insulin dependent), seizure disorder, and chronic arthritic pain in lower back and both knees. Her mother showed beginning stages of Alzheimer's, high blood pressure, diabetes (insulin dependent) and was a breast cancer survivor having a mastectomy performed about ten years earlier.

Pat, attending to her parent's needs from a distance, quickly assessed that their physical health, personal hygiene and ability to maintain basic housekeeping functions, were unsafe and life-threatening.

My wife assessed that her mother's deteriorating cognitive abilities as a homemaker became nonexistent. This fact became clearly evident when Pat's dad asked his wife to bring him a cup of ice water. What his wife returned with was an eye-opener—a cup filled with frozen french fries!

Pat's dad was never the homemaker. The mother, an excellent homemaker, was always the stay-at-home mom that had raised five children. Pat's dad tried to take over homemaker duties, but it was extremely difficult for him to manage and maintain. His homemaker role consisted of ordering for delivery take-out food consisting of sandwiches (subs/hoagies), pizza, or occasionally going to local buffet-style restaurants.

Their morning breakfast routine frequently consisted of eating supermarket pastries, having tea and toast, and occasionally drinking coffee. Little or no effort was given to either managing their nutritional intake for diabetes or doing basic household chores like cleaning, washing dishes, and doing laundry. The house was always a mess with piled-up dishes, soiled paper plates, pizza boxes, and soda or ice tea containers scattered all over the house.

Her father's obstinacy for not having caregivers come into the home to provide basic health and homemaking care services was an issue for her to resolve from a distance. This was especially evident as she spent countless hours making arrangements for basic health and homemaker care services in the home only to find out later her dad had cancelled services.

Pat's dad insisted the service was not necessary. "Don't spend the money. I can handle it." Her dad, a GI-generation prodigy, was very frugal with his funds, living through both the Depression and World War II.

Pat would spend every weekend traveling to New Jersey to clean their kitchen and bathroom. She would prepare meals for the week, wash and fold clothes, wash dishes, take out the trash, and empty food containers that were piled up during the week. She would monitor and dispense their week's worth of medications in pill containers and prefill insulin syringes.

Pat's sister-in-law, living in the same town as her dad, would check on them daily during the week. She did light shopping for them, checked mail, paid their bills, and reminded them of upcoming doctor appointments. The sister-in-law would also help change the mother's soiled clothes and often bathe her. The sister-in-law would monitor pill containers of daily medication and insulin use and would report back to Pat any unusual behaviors.

During this time, life was very stressful for Pat managing two family households, Delaware and New Jersey, while I was relocated in Georgia. Both of us decided it would be best for her to stay in Delaware until the house was sold and our daughter graduated from high school.

When, I couldn't always fly home, I would call Pat, checking in to see how she fared with her parents. She would frequently complain about her dad's stubbornness, paranoia, and laziness. This made managing their life extremely difficult.

Eventually her dad came to his senses, asking and wanting help attending to his wife. Pat's mother, during that time, was having frequent episodes of wandering off alone. Her dad, having difficulty walking with knees and back problem, would often handle the situation by calling Pat and telling her, "Your mother has wandered off again."

One particular incident that caught his attention was her wandering off in the neighborhood, which resulted in a serious fall injury. That particular incident resulted in her being hospitalized. That was the breakthrough for her dad to finally cave in and ask for help and assistance.

Finally, Pat began making immediate plans with her dad to have them move to Georgia once we sold our house in Delaware. Pat's dad was very supportive of the initial move to Georgia; however, we later found out he was planning a secondary secret mission.

Chapter 3

The Crossroad Challenge

Living Healthy or Living Carnally: Ensuring a Future Lifestyle of Independence

What's making baby boomers and young adults seriously ill today? What's contributing to many people's ill health that will eventually lead them to seek a caregiver? The question many young adults should ask themselves is, "What practicing lifestyle will ensure my future life's independence and wellness at fifty and beyond?"

The shocking reality for many people is that lifestyle choices and decisions for living healthy or living carnally are predicated by two things: (1) parents' decisions and health choices and (2) lifestyle choices, decisions, and practices you embrace in adulthood. Living healthy or carnally starts early in life. It's a personal course of action-- choosing to stay healthy or live carnally (unhealthy). The choice is simple: live healthy for the harsh reality. Someday in your distant future, you will be unable to care for yourself.

Let's take a critical look at people's modern-day lifestyle challenges for aging in place and then discuss mechanisms causing unhealthy outcomes. Lifestyle and environmental mechanisms often are potent factors leading to health and wellness or adverse, unhealthy outcomes.

First, three key terms need to be defined: *lifestyle, living healthy*, and *carnal living.* Lifestyle is a reflection of your individual identity expressed by attitudes, beliefs, and behaviors. In simple terms, these are your personal values and habits. A healthy lifestyle, therefore, focuses on values and how nutritional choices, eating habits, and environment determines health outcomes and longevity.

The term *living healthy* is your correlating actions. Living healthy is the attitudes, beliefs, and behaviors for exercising intelligent lifestyle choices for a better quality of life. It is a state of wellness. It is the complete state of physical, mental, and social well-being by exercising intelligent choices to prevent or manage adverse health outcomes.

Carnal living is simply a personal desire or motivation to pursue the dictates of the flesh. It is an addiction whereby your values and choices are emotionally influenced and controlled by the body's desires. These desires are habit-forming behaviors leading toward a destructive pathway.

Here begins the challenge for many people and the first critical aging-in-place lifestyle lesson. An unhealthy lifestyle is the root cause for poor health outcomes. People must begin to live and practice a healthy lifestyle early in life. The end result we all should strive for is to living healthy. The outcome measure will allow you to maintain your independence and not become a liability on your family.

Many want to age gracefully to live out a life with health intact to go places and to stay in one's own home and community. The harsh reality for most people is not being able to do so. Why? You have not taken appropriate actions when you were young to make health and wellness a top practicing lifestyle.

The challenge confronting many today is focusing on lifestyle values and individual choices and recognizing environment challenges that impact health and wellness. How you manage your lifestyle early in life is key to aging gracefully with mind, health, and physical mobility intact. The consequence of an unhealthy lifestyle is simple: you someday will need a caregiver(s) to look after you.

Unhealthy Lifestyles Contribute to People Needing Caregivers

The pathway of an unhealthy lifestyle eventually leads to poor health, institutionalization, disability, and early death. The goal is *practicing a lifelong lifestyle behavior of living healthy to age gracefully*. The long-term lifestyle outcome is to age in place keeping both health and cognitive abilities fully functional and intact so that you can live independently in the comforts of your own home and community.

Table 1 shows key lifestyle risk factors impacting health, wellness, and future caregiver dependency. Living healthy is a lifelong practicing behavior in wellness. It's a commitment to a lifestyle regimen to avoid risky behaviors leading to unhealthy outcomes.

Therefore, the first steps to age in place are becoming aware of key risk factors and mechanisms that are the central root of the problem. These key factors can be summarized into two simple terms—intrinsic and extrinsic lifestyle mechanisms.

An intrinsic lifestyle is the personal behaviors and habits you can personally control. Simply, you can accomplish this lifestyle just by living healthy and avoiding risky behaviors that lead to accidents, injuries, and adverse health outcomes. Chapter 8 will discuss these in more detail.

Table 2 shows extrinsic mechanisms contributing to poor health outcomes. These are factors that many of you are not aware of or choose not to become informed about. These are serious mechanisms, often subtle in scope, that have dangerous and long-term consequences on our health and environment.

An example of an extrinsic factor is cigarette smoking. Smoking and its effects of lung cancer are fully documented as hazardous to one's health. Likewise, other intrinsic and extrinsic mechanisms (see tables below) are other modern-day health hazards that will also have an impact on health, wellness, and well-being to age-in-place.

Table 1

Common Intrinsic Factors Leading to Caregiving Dependency/Services
Chronic disease conditions
Unintentional fall-related Injury
Traumatic brain or spinal cord injury
Cognitive health: Alzheimer's disease, dementia, Parkinson's disease, mental health and psychiatric disorders

Table II

Common Extrinsic Factors Affecting Health and Wellness
Science and technology
Contamination from industrial pollutants into the environment
Genetically modified organisms (GMOs) in food supply
Chemical contaminants in home and other products (toys, plastics, bottled water)
Medical science drugs and antibiotics

In an effort to live healthy to age-in-place we must now consider these other mechanisms that are impacting our overall state of health and wellness. Later in this book, I will discuss in more detail these modern-day hazards for living healthy to stay healthy.

Finally, has profit run amok over consumer health and safety interest to live and to stay healthy? Have government regulations offered adequate protection and safeguards? And how have climate change and big business affected the environment? I see the reckoning crisis looming ahead, and all of us will someday need caregivers. Living healthy to avoid a life of becoming a dependent may not be ours to control unless we truly educate ourselves about making health and wellness a top priority.

The Caregiver Conundrum—Aging and Lifestyle

Now that I have your attention, let's turn the focus to baby boomers and especially young adults at the inevitable life crossroads. We will all need to begin formulating plans in these modern days to care for ourselves to age-in-place. The crossroads challenge facing many of you in these coming days is the reckoning that some of you are already family caregivers, and for others, you will someday need caregiving.

The crossroads I speak about have two distinct life pathways. In one direction running both ways, we have a lifestyle lane of old age with no easy pass. The other direction running both ways, east and west, is our lifestyle express lane of choices. Unfortunately at the crossroad of old age and lifestyle, there are neither traffic signals nor traffic guards at the intersection.

Life has no set timetable for the inevitable life incidences coming your way. Many of you choosing a pathway may get there aging safely with health, mind, and memory intact. Others getting to the crossroads may encounter lifestyle obstacles such as unhealthy outcomes that lead to poor health and people needing both caregiving and caregivers.

A critical look at health crossroad contributing to both old age and lifestyle should first look at old age and its myths and facts about aging. Old age is not a disease. It is a process of physical, psychological, and social changes over time. Old-age aging as a secondary mechanism is also exacerbated by trauma and disease.

Generally, family caregivers usually care for children and the elderly with an injury or chronic disease illness that has impacted their activity of daily living. Many believe old age is the reason for ill or failing health. Simply, there is an old-age myth to dispel here. Old age should not be given as a reason for ill health. It's an inability to live healthy as a top lifestyle priority to gracefully age-in-place.

Here, life's crossroad takes a directional path where good and bad choices are made. The directional pathway we choose early in life will eventually determine our health outcomes and ability to age gracefully in place.

The pathway for aging gracefully is *living healthy*, with health, mind, and memories intact. The other pathway choice is a carnal lifestyle, with no cares or restraints as to the negative effects this lifestyle will have on you, your family, and your finances as you age. An unhealthy, carnal lifestyle will lead to addictions, disease, early death, and disability in the future.

Dispelling the Myths about Aging[1]

Illness is an expectation of just growing old.

> Illness should not be expected nor accepted as a symptom of growing old. Changing lifestyle and behaviors can prevent many adverse health outcomes.

1　Lingren, H. G. *Questions & Answer: Myths and Fact about Aging.* Hawaii Institute for Tropical Agriculture and Human Resources, 2006.

Thinking processes become slower and less sharp once a person reaches sixty-five and older.

> Lapses in memory occur anytime when the brain is not constantly challenged. Also, less information reaches the brain as vision and hearing become less sensitive.

Older adult workers miss more time from work because of health illness than young people.

> Older adult workers work more efficiently and miss less work because of illness and are on time more often than younger workers.

Older adults eighty-five and older will be unable to maintain an active and independent lifestyle because of a chronic disease condition.

> Most chronic ailments for which treatment is available are manageable in older adults. About eighty percent of persons over age eighty-five can carry out all daily living activities.

Older adults will be widowed before the age of seventy-five.

> About eighty percent of elderly married women and twenty percent of elderly married men must adjust to being widowed at some point before age seventy-five.

Most older adults are expected to live the remaining years of their lives in a nursing home.

> Only five percent of persons over age sixty-five are in nursing homes, and only twenty percent of those over eighty-five require such care.

A healthy living and wellness lifestyle can slow the effects of aging.

Diet, exercise, substance-free habits, intellectual activity, meaningful social relationships, and a sense of purpose can prolong vitality and prevent or postpone adverse health outcomes and disability.

SECTION II
The Conundrum!

The Modern-Day Family-Caregiving Crisis

A health care system that relies on untrained and unpaid family members to perform skilled medical/nursing tasks, but does not train and support them, has lost sight of its primary mission of providing humane and compassionate care to sick people and their families.

—"A Study Report: How Professionals and Caregivers Can Help Each Other"
United Hospital Fund and the AARP Public Policy Institute

CHAPTER 4

Expanding the Family Household

One Small Act Can Make a Big Difference
—John C. Maxwell

Distant to Full-Time Caregiver and the In-Laws (Part 3)

Pat and I decided, after many heartfelt discussions, that her parents' future for living independently in New Jersey was no longer an option. They would have to come live with us once we found a place in Georgia. My family situation was still in a state of influx, for Pat was trying to sell the Delaware residence and trying desperately to not uproot our youngest daughter in her senior year of high school.

I began looking in Georgia for a home with enough space to accommodate her parents. After many visits looking at many neighborhoods for that perfect home to accommodate *us*, we finally agreed that with her parents' financial help, it would be best to expand the family living accommodations and household and build a custom home.

Many home plans were searched and reviewed, looking for suitable floor plan space that could easily be remodeled to include an in-law suite. Once the floor plan was determined,

I sought and identified an excellent building contractor with experience in multigenerational housing modification.

The next step with the building contractor was to bring into the process the services of a home interior designer specializing in home environments with universal design features (see section IV, chapter 13). Floor plans were redrawn, incorporating universal design features in the floor plan design. The goal and intent was to allow Pat's parents to live independently.

Pat's life, once the decision was made to relocate her parents, went from part-time distant caregiver to full-time unpaid family caregiver. The decision to move them was not entirely unexpected. Pat and I had a premonition in the late 1980s that someday in the distant future we would have to care for one or both of our parents. We also both realized that the move to Georgia was a benevolent gesture, but it also meant we would be distant and recluse of frequent help and support from any immediate family.

Pat took on the challenge in 2003 to have them move to Georgia. In hindsight, while there were many obstacles and logistics planning their move, in hindsight, the move was an eye-opening elder care learning experience.

Making the decision to become an in-home family caregiver wasn't an easy decision to make. The valuable lessons we both learned from this experience were numerous, but the most significant lessons we took away from this lifestyle caregiving experience was the reckoning:

- ❖ Someday in the not-so-distant future, you will need a caregiver!
- ❖ A medical illness and chronic disease conditions can cause a lifestyle disability, hampering one's mental and physical ability to live independently.

❖ Begin early developing your own smart family plans to age-in-place.

Note: developing your smart family plans to age-in-place will be discussed in section IV and V of this book.

The In-Law Family Story and the Move

The move from southern New Jersey to Atlanta, Georgia, began in 2003. The first lesson that became quite clear was her dad's cognitive impairment was more noticeable as we spent more time with him. Pat, so we thought, drew up a brilliant plan to move her parents to Georgia. Her dad finally agreed to the move, so we devised a plan to move them during the Fourth of July holiday. Planning the move to relocate them required us to address the one major obstacle standing in the way: her mom was not going to get on a plane to fly.

The plan we carefully devised was to drive two cars to Georgia. The plan was to drive south in two cars alternating among three drivers, driving his Cadillac and a rental car that I rented in Georgia and drove to New Jersey. Pat made arrangements with her dad to get his car a tune-up, oil change, and other mechanical system checked before the trip. Her dad wanted to take his car to Georgia as part of his conditions with Pat for them to move.

Her mom, clearly showing early signs of dementia, was totally unaware of the pending trip. Riding in his car for her would be a familiar routine since Pat's dad drove many times to Delaware while I was assigned there (fourteen years).

The plan to move took shape when I rented a car in late June in Georgia and drove up to southern New Jersey. The plan was for all of us to travel together, taking turns as drivers, driving two cars back to Georgia. The plan was simple: spend one night in a hotel in Delaware and one night in North Carolina and take the final journey to Georgia.

This was all carefully planned to not bring unnecessary attention to Pat's mother that we were permanently moving to Georgia. Her mother was only told we were going to spend a few days in Delaware for the holidays. Looking back on the move, she seemed contented for she only complained once: "When are we going to get there?"

The In-Law—Lost on the Way

The first of July, we began our journey leaving New Jersey to travel south. Pat decided to only pack their medicine, toiletries, and nothing else. New clothes were purchased just for the trip. All other clothing and essentials would be bought when we arrived in Georgia.

During the first phase of the trip, a planned stop and layover in Delaware, we encountered our first major problem—car problems with the Cadillac. That afternoon, Pat, her dad, and I drew up a plan for the following day to take his car to a nearby automotive dealership to be repaired.

The next day, her dad and I got up early to take his car to the dealership. Pat's dad took his car as planned, and he followed me in the rental car, a large SUV-size vehicle. The plan was to drop his car off at the dealership and for us to return back to the hotel to eat breakfast.

Holy moly, on the way to the dealership from the hotel, her dad took an inadvertent wrong turn off Delaware Highway US Route 13 and I lost sight of him in my rearview mirror. Trying not to panic, I found a place to make a U-turn in the morning rush hour traffic. When I turned around, I proceeded to backtrack to where I thought he might have gone. Now, I was in panic mode. All I could think of was what I was going to tell Pat: "I lost your dad."

After looking for about ten minutes, which seemed like hours, I finally broke down, pulled over on the side of the road near Delaware State University, and called Pat to inform her about the bad news. She replied with a harsh tone, *"What do you mean you lost my dad?"* I calmly explained to her I lost him. He took a wrong turn not following me!

The conversation with Pat took several minutes, but it seemed like an eternity. We conversed with each other for several minutes when my second panic attack came on. Looking in my rearview mirror, I saw flashing lights. Yes, I suddenly became a focus of the state police.

Now the police was involved, questioning me about parking on the shoulder highway of a university. I proceeded to mention that I lost my father-in-law, who was following me to a dealership. I informed the police officer he was elderly and was unfamiliar with the area.

The police officer turned his focus away from me to my father-in-law. He started asking me a lot of questions about Pat's father. Did he have a cell phone? Did he have my number or his daughter's number? Did he know the hotel where we were staying?

One of many answers startled the officer, but there was one particular reply I politely answered: *"Yes, he does have a cell phone, but he may not know how to use it."* Yikes, what did I say that for? The police officer must have been thinking to himself, an old man driving around town with a cognitive disability. I thought I was toast. The police officer took my information and the hotel we were staying and radioed the call to the dispatcher to locate a car and my father-in-law—missing in Delaware.

When I arrived back at the hotel, Pat was already calling family members back home in New Jersey. She hoped that her dad might have called a family member back home. Hours seemed to quickly pass with no word, no calls, nothing, and her dad still missing in action. I went back out on the road again, looking around town and nearby dealerships, still trying to locate him.

Finally after hours had passed, my wife called, telling me they had located him. Pat informed me that an auto repair shop, far on the west side of town, called her brother back in New Jersey. They told her that their dad was waiting in their lobby for his car to be repaired.

Leaving for the auto shop, I circled back to the hotel to pick up Pat and her mother. Upon our arrival to the repair shop Mr. Jones was patiently waiting in the lobby, unconcerned and unfazed by the circumstances of events. His only concern was what could be the problem with his car.

Pat's dad had found a repair shop, checked in the car, gave his New Jersey address and an old landline telephone number that was disconnected. He did not provide the receptionist with his own cell phone number. He did, however, discuss with the auto mechanic the issues he was having with the car.

The receptionist at the auto shop quickly assessed that something wasn't right when she noticed he was making no effort to call someone to pick him up. The repair shop told Pat's dad that it would take some time to diagnose the problem with the car. When the receptionist asked again if someone was going to pick him up, his reply raised more suspicion that he needed help.

The receptionist asked again if she could call someone to pick him up. He then informed her that he was traveling with his daughter and wife to Georgia. When she asked him if he had a cell phone to contact anyone, he pulled his cell phone from his pocket and gave it to the receptionist.

His cell phone was turned off at the time, preventing anyone from contacting him. The receptionist took the phone, turned it on, and asked him if there was a number she could call for him. Although all our numbers were programmed in his cell phone directory, he could only recall by memory his son's telephone number back in New Jersey. The receptionist called that number and spoke to his son, informing him that his dad was waiting there at the auto repair shop. His son called Pat, and the mystery of the father-in-law missing in Delaware was solved.

Pat asked her dad why he inadvertently made a wrong turn, not following me to the dealership. His reply was "I thought I was following the right person by focusing on the back of his head."

The trip, we later concluded, was the first of many incidences that made us begin to seriously take notice of her dad's cognitive disability. Her dad, we later assessed, was a master at concealing his disabilities. In hindsight, the trip made us keenly aware of the depth of his cognitive dysfunction.

The Arrival and the Beginning of an Extended-Family Lifestyle

The move was just the first of many enormous tasks Pat had to undertake as the principal caregiver. Now taking on a full-time role of an unpaid in-home parent caregiver, a new lifestyle emerged. The shocking reality upon their arrival in Georgia, was finding out how bad her parents' conditions had become physically and mentally.

The first immediate challenge was getting their health properly managed and controlled. This was quite a challenge, trying to get them to cultivate a healthier new lifestyle behavior at their age. Her mother's dementia was the easy one to manage and get under control. Her dad being obstinate, cantankerous, and lazy, was the difficult one to convince to change old lifestyle habits like moving off sweets and pastries.

Pat's first order of business and most difficult task was piecing together their medical record history for the past fifteen to twenty years. Her parents' dementia did not make the task easy. My wife was able to assemble information from old pill bottles and physicians' names to obtain records and medical histories.

Pat then was able to piece together medical histories and timelines of hospital visits and medical procedures they both received. In the process, Pat was able to piece together ten-year medical histories and information about medical specialists seen throughout the tri-state region (Pennsylvania, New Jersey, and Delaware).

Because both parents had dementia, they could not clearly recall names of specific physician specialists they had seen over the years. Pat's mom and dad both knew the name of their primary care doctor, for he had been a longtime practicing physician in the local county. Her dad frequently went to the Veterans Administration Hospital to receive his medical care. His visits left a clear paper trail of referrals to other physicians and hospital visits for surgical procedures performed.

The second order of business was getting her dad's frequent medical problems properly managed and under control. When her dad arrived in Georgia, we noticed he started to display frequent unexplained symptoms of dizziness after eating.

He was getting weaker after eating, losing strength, and falling frequently. His frequent falls became more difficult to manage because his weight, hovering around three hundred pounds, made it damn near impossible to pick himself up off the floor without assistance. Finally, due to his frequent falls, we solved the falling problem by purchasing a patient Hoyer Lift to aid us in getting him up off the floor.

The mystery of his condition was puzzling, and his falls were becoming more frequent after each meal. Finally, it was advised to uncover this mystery of weakness and frequent falls. The next fall incident, Pat decided that we should have him transported to the hospital for a complete fall-injury evaluation and workup. Upon the visit to the ER, they admitted him to the hospital and doctors were able to identify a toxicity to a seizure medication he had been taking for many years.

The next step in this process was to find and schedule new area physicians. This was not an easy process, for we first relied on friends known in the area for referrals and recommendations. This was a challenge because many physicians referred to us by other people did not particularly specialize in elder care matters.

Pat took on the meticulous task of finding new physicians and specialists. Her medical assessment as a nurse determined that her parents needed a plethora of doctors, including care for eyes, feet, teeth, skin, and diabetes medical specialists. This was an arduous task in itself, for it was time-consuming.

The process of finding new physicians took about a year before Pat was satisfied with their doctors and level of care. Also, the process of getting her dad's Delaware VA records transferred and re-enrolled at the Georgia Veterans Administration under a new medical team was another challenge. I dare not say how long that took!

Truly, this is my family story, sandwiched in a modern-day caregiving lifestyle crisis. The important lesson to take away from this is simply, "*One* small act can make a difference." My wife, in this case, made a significant difference, for I dare say without her intervention, her parents' lives would have been short-lived.

Chapter 5

The Reckoning Crisis by the Numbers

> *Eighty (80%) of long-term care giving is performed by unpaid caregivers, often a family member, friend or neighbor who receives no financial compensation.*
> —Alzheimer's Association

The Family Caregiver's Lifestyle Crisis

The first of many family-caregiving crises in these modern days is in the area of in-home, long-term care provided by an unpaid family member, usually a spouse, relative, child, or friend. While modern medicine has increased life expectancy for many adults, there still remains the question, "Can or will you be able to live out your remaining years in the comfort of your own home?"

The critical question looming ahead for many people in this modern-day era is, "While people are living longer, have you formulated a plan to help care for you or aging parents' future senior-care needs?" Have you and your spouse talked about an aging-in-place plan? And what family member can or will care for you and your spouse in your time of need?

Many sandwich generations, baby boomers, and especially young adults will soon be entrenched in a family-caregiving crossroads, needing help. Who will provide that help? And are state/local government and business leaders prepared for this fast-growing, aging population tsunami?

The reckoning crisis looming ahead for many people is now here, like a tsunami ready to engulf us. Simply, in this modern-day society of living a hectic lifestyle, many people have not paid attention to planning their future senior-care needs when health, cognitive skills, and physical abilities erode. As a society, many people have not made a proactive family plan to age in place. Why?

Pushing this reckoning crisis involves four major points of contentions:

- ❖ Longer life expectancy for adults. The staggering growth of baby boomers turning sixty-five each day will continue until 2030.
- ❖ Eating to live healthy. Foods can be the safest source of nutrition or the slowest form of poison.
- ❖ An unhealthy lifestyle affects quality of life. Health and wellness are not considered a top lifestyle priority.
- ❖ Huge shortage of skilled professional caregivers and unskilled in-home caregivers will not match the future demand for services.[2]

Our current modern-day lifestyle is cultivating a destructive pathway for unhealthy outcomes and future caregiving dependency. The caregiving crisis, which I call the day of reckoning, unfold here for sandwich generations. What plans are you pursuing to live healthy and better to stay independent?

---

2 Dill, Michael J., and Edward S. Salsberg. *The Complexities of Physician Supply and Demand: Projections Through 2025.* Association of American Medical Colleges, 2008

Living an unhealthy lifestyle is a quick pathway to unhealthy outcomes. Practicing a lifestyle of unhealthy behaviors will lead to someone caring for you someday. Who will take on this role of an in-home, long-term-care, family caregiver when health and memory erode? What immediate sibling may be willing and committed to take on caregiving roles, duties, and responsibilities?

Finally, will there be enough professionally trained caregivers and long-term care institutions to handle the expected demand? Will there be enough in-home service workers, homemakers, and aides to meet the expected tsunami of baby boomers and future generations?

The Reckoning by the Numbers

First, the growth in the number of baby boomers will combine to double the population of Americans aged sixty-five and older during the next seventeen years. Statistics show that eight thousand to ten thousand baby boomers from now until 2030 will turn sixty-five each day. That's one person every ten seconds.

Second, working as a family caregiver doesn't pay well. The work as a family caregiver is demanding, stressful, and dangerous. According to the Alzheimer's Association, eighty percent, 80% of long-term care giving is performed by unpaid caregivers, often a family member, friend, or neighbor who receives no financial compensation

Third, there undoubtedly will be a shortage of both skilled and unskilled professional health care workers as the industry reckons with the explosion of aging baby boomers. According to a 2008 report from the Association of American Medical Colleges (AAMC), the American Hospital Association (AHA)

and other industry groups project a substantial shortage of skilled health care professionals[3].

The study project also cites the following:

- ❖ A skilled health care professional workforce shortage with the implementation of the Affordable Care Act.
- In future years an estimated shortage of at least 155,000 physicians and 500,000 nurses are expected before 2025. [4]
- ❖ Similar professional shortages are projected for other healthcare fields including but not limited to mental health, public health, and dental providers.

Health professionals retiring and the additional thirty-two million people expecting to seek health care services as a result of the Affordable Care Act will stretch the health care workforce thin. Also impacting this crisis is the unprecedented increase of chronic disease conditions among all populations and age groups.

According to the Centers for Disease Control (CDC), seventy-five percent of the nation's health care dollars go to the treatment of chronic diseases. These persistent conditions like high blood pressure, cancer, stroke, heart attack, diabetes, obesity, and many more are the nation's leading causes of death and lifelong disability that compromises individual's quality of life.

---

3   "A Substantial Shortage of Skilled Care Professionals", Association of American Medical Colleges (AAMC), American Hospital Association (AHA), 2008.

4   Dill, Michael J., and Edward S. Salsberg. *The Complexities of Physician Supply and Demand: Projections Through 2025*. Association of American Medical Colleges, 2008

A 2004 CDC study shows about one in every four people with chronic conditions has one or more daily activity limitations[5]. A daily activity limitation includes assistance needed for dressing, eating, ambulation, toiletry, and hygiene to maintain quality of life. What chronic disease condition may negatively impact your quality of life?

Central to the burgeoning healthcare costs for sandwich generations are three other key driving factors pushing the caregiving crisis:

(1) Preventing/managing chronic disease conditions
(2) Maintaining cognitive health functions
(3) Preventing fall injuries among older adults

Later in the book, I will address these aforementioned issues in more detail, but one must also infer other revelations:

(4) The future unskilled workforce for middle-class working families needing in-home family caregivers (health and homemaker aides) will most likely come from racial/ethnic minority populations.
(5) Government officials must resolve our immigration problem with a sensible pathway to citizenship that will allow institutions to tap into this undocumented large workforce.

I hope that in some way, my life experiences, both as a retired public health professional and unpaid family caregiver, will help you plan your future for staying in your home. Looking ahead, people must first start formulating an in-home, long-term-care, aging-in-place plan to stay and age in their own homes and communities.

---

5   Anderson, G. Chronic Conditions: Making the Case for Ongoing Care. Baltimore: John Hopkins University, 2004.

The second point to this caregiving crisis is making health a lifestyle priority. Living and practicing a healthy lifestyle early on in life will allow you to maintain independence in your senior years. Many people will surely need a caregiver or caregivers to care for them. The question for many is, "Who will that be--sibling, family member, friend, neighbor, or institutional facility?"

The point of reckoning for sandwich generations begins here with awareness. Who will care for you? And have you made your in-home, long-term-care, smart family plan to age-in-place?

Assessing Risks for Future Caregiver Dependency—Quiz

Let's see if you will need a caregiver(s) in the distant future. Take this brief exercise so that you may become aware of your own modern-day lifestyle challenges for living healthy to stay independent.

After this exercise, read on, and the book will address in other chapters the seven core components for formulating your own in-home, long-term-care, smart family plans to age in place.

Please take the time to take this simple quiz assessing your family situation, personal health, and lifestyle risk. If you answer yes to any of the following questions, you may already be pursuing a lifestyle pathway causing you to someday need a caregiver(s).

Assessing Family and Lifestyle Risks: Will You Need a Caregiver(s)?

Risk Challenges	Place a check mark [yes] if indicated
Are you currently providing caregiver duties and services for a family member or friend (distant or in home)?	
Do you provide care for an adult child or grandkid (with or without special needs)?	
Are you contemplating within the next three to five years taking on in-home family-caregiver duties/responsibilities for a family member (parent), relative, or friend?	
Are you an only sibling?	
Do you have family siblings who most likely cannot be counted upon to assume caregiver duties for you or your spouse?	
Do you have a family history of diabetes, heart disease, stroke, or obesity?	
Do you personally have a chronic disease condition/illness? (*See appendix A for complete list of conditions.*)	
Do you have extra belly fat? (For females, is your waist circumference greater than thirty-five inches? For males, is your waist circumference greater than forty inches?)	
Are you inactive (not exercising at least thirty minutes four times a week)?	
Is your mental sharpness or memory not what it used to be?	
Are you experiencing dwindling personal finances, from retirement, forced early retirement, debt, children returning home, caring for grandkids, medical issues, etc.?	
Do you plan to stay in your home when you retire (i.e., aging-in-place)?	
Is your home presently not suitable to live in as you get older? (Think about aging-in-place home modifications that will need to be made.)	

Scoring Key

Once you have completed the exercise, go ahead and add up your total points. The scoring chart below will assess your potential lifestyle risk for someday needing a caregiver(s).

The goal of this exercise is for you to think ahead and set forth an action strategy for aging in place. The exercise is not intended to be a scientific survey. It is intended to just give you a snapshot of your future aging lifestyle challenges and to show you that you need to begin formulating your own smart family plans to age in place. Someday in the not-so-distant future, you will need a caregiver(s). So who will be caring for you?

Score Assessment Chart

Score	Challenge	Individual Action	Aging-in-Place Strategy
1–4	Not there yet: just entering the caregiver crossroad.	Open family dialogue about in-home caregiving.	Not there yet: continue reading.
5–8	Time is of the essence.	Talk to family members about your aging-in-place needs.	Begin formulating your smart family plans for aging in place.
9+	Critical: you will need a caregiver in your distant future. Who?	Identify a family member as your in-home caregiver and care manager.	Make and finalize smart family plans for aging in place.

Chapter 6

Sandwich Generations Engulfed in a Lifestyle of Family Caregiving

Nearly 44 million Americans, 1 in 5 adults, are unpaid family caregivers for a parent, relative or friend over age 50.
—"Caregiving in the US"
The National Alliance for Caregiving and AARP, 2009

The New-Aged Generations of Family Caregivers

They're three population generations that are currently sandwiched in a real life crisis of caregiving for family members and friends. Population Generations making up this untrained workforce of family caregivers are: Baby Boomers; Generation X; and Generation Y population -- young adults, sometime called Millennials.

Previously outlined in an earlier chapter were the many crossroad challenges population generations will have to content with over the next two next decades. From the increasing growth of baby boomers turning 65; huge professional shortage of both skilled and unskilled healthcare personnel; and the increasing incidences of chronic disease conditions, causing disability and impaired quality of life — all point to an impending crisis.

The new challenge, population generations now face is being sandwiched in a lifestyle of expanded family caregiving. The additional crisis now engulf the lives of families showing increasing numbers -- 1 in 5 adults are now sandwiched in an expanded family lifestyle of caregiving.

Are you ready? .... Are families prepared to handle this crisis? At the center of this caregiving plight are these three population generations. They are -- or soon will be -- sandwiched in a lifestyle-stage caring for parents, grandparents, family relatives, children, and grandchildren?

First, baby boomers, born 1947–1964, are at the forefront of this caregiving reckoning crisis. Baby boomers are the principal generation caring for older parents, children, and grandkids. Second, generation X, born 1965–1979, who have finished college, are working, are married with adult children, or are single and childless have taken on an expanded lifestyle of caregiving by default. The youngest female siblings of boomers are usually the primary family caregivers recruited.

Millennials, born 1980–2000, are the techie generation, immersed in modern-day technology and gadgetry, and are trying to establish their own careers. They are most likely college educated, career oriented, debt-ridden, and struggling raising their own children. Some are attending to a parent or favorite family relative, usually from a distance. This generation, because of life's circumstances, may not be there for you in your time of need.

The Term "Sandwich Generations" (Principal Family Caregivers)

The term *sandwich generations*[6] is a term coined by Dorothy Miller in 1981. The term refers to people who are caught up in a

---

6 Miller, D. "The 'Sandwich' Generation: Adult Children of the Aging." Social Work, no. 26 (1981): 419–423.

lifestyle stage, caring for their aging parents or grandparents. In most instances, they feel some remorse for not giving full support for their own children. These three generations especially are our unpaid family caregivers. They're the principal modern-day workforce and our future stakeholders.

According to the Pew Research Center, just over one of every eight Americans aged forty to sixty is both raising a child and caring for a parent. In addition, between seven to ten million adults care for their aging parents from a distance. The guilt and emotional swings of these generations of unpaid family caregivers are enormous.

Baby boomers are at the forefront of this caregiving crisis. Baby boomers who care for their aging parents are now saddled with additional responsibilities of caring for and raising their grandchildren. According to Carol Abaya in featured articles --*The Sandwich Generation*[7], she categorizes the caregiving generation as:

> Traditional sandwich: those sandwiched between aging parents who need care or help and are caring for their own children;
>
> Club sandwich: those in their fifties and sixties who are sandwiched between aging parents, adult children, and grandchildren; or those in their thirties and forties with young children, aging parents, and grandparents;
>
> Open-faced sandwich: anyone else involved in elder care.

---

7 Abaya, Carol. *The Sandwich Generation*, thesandwichgeneration.com

The Unpaid Family Caregiver—a Lifestyle Ministry

Chances are if you are a caregiver for a family member / friend or you are contemplating the roles, duties, and responsibilities of a family caregiver, you have been thrust into the role as a caregiver for a parent and you should be commended for your service into a lifestyle ministry of caregiving.

Let's be clear. Not everyone is qualified for this ministry of caregiving, and not everyone is up to the lifestyle challenges of coping with finances, guilt, grief, time, and exhaustion that come with the job. Finally, not everyone has the temperament to be a family caregiver.

A family caregiver is a family member, relative, or friend that usually helps an individual with his or her activities for daily living. Activities for daily living *(ADL)* is a healthcare term used to refer to daily self-care activities within the individual's place of residence (home). ADLs are things we do for a person who otherwise cannot or has difficulty doing those things for himself or herself.

Typically, ADL activities involve basic functions of eating, bathing, dressing, toileting, and ambulation – walking with or without the use of an assistive device [e.g., walker, cane, crutches or using a wheelchair]. Additional challenges for the family caregiver are rearranging work schedules in order to accommodate visiting nurses and therapists coming to the home. They ensure that food is prepared for times when they are not at home due to extra school activities or work travel assignments.

> *Unpaid family caregiver (UPFC):* a family member, relative, or friend that usually helps an individual (loved one) with his or her activities for daily living. These activities usually involve basic functions such as eating, bathing, dressing, toiletry, and ambulation (walking assistance).

Another type of caregiver is a family member that helps with a person's *instrumental activities for daily living (IADL)*. IDAL includes paying bills, shopping, preparing meals, housekeeping, managing medications, and making doctor appointments. These activities are often performed by one family member or distributed among family members, relatives, and friends.

Family members involved in the aforementioned activities often perform some of these activities from a distance. A person assuming these duties and responsibilities usually arranges, coordinates, and collaborates with other family members, health care professionals, and service providers as a facilitator to manage their affairs.

While most people think that family caregivers are persons who care for elderly parents or spouses, an unpaid family caregiver may also care for children with special needs. Special-needs people are children or adults with serious mental or physical disabilities.

The family caregiver who cares for people with serious mental or physical disabilities is a special caregiver. They are special individuals who have a unique skill set that is more labor-intensive than that of general caregivers. These special caregivers carry out duties without much fanfare and appreciation and should be given special thanks for the ministry they perform. They are truly the gifted individuals in the life ministry of family caregiving.

Table 1

The Unpaid Family Caregiver Lifestyle Routine

Typical
        ADL functions

Enhanced
        Transportation
        Housework (cleaning and removing clutter)

Grocery shopping
Preparing meals
Managing parent's finances
Helping with medications (administering and monitoring)
Arranging medical or senior service appointments
Arranging contractual services

Finally, the unpaid family caregiver is usually charged with making living arrangements comfortable or close to what was provided at the parent's prior residence. They will purchase equipment such as a patient lift-chair or recliner, mattress covers and pads, a shower chair, and more, which is all part of caregiving duties.

In addition, hiring professional contractors for placement of safety bars, making bathrooms wheelchair accessible, installing access ramps and other universal design household features are important tasks. Note, universal design will be described in more detail in Section IV—Environmental Home Modification Health and Safety Strategies.

Sandwiched into Service—The DeCosta Story

The DeCosta family is a two-parent household with three children. The family's oldest child is in high school, one is in elementary school, and the youngest child just turned two. Both parents work full-time with flexible schedules to work from home. They lead a normal modern-day lifestyle that involves typical after-school activities with their children.

Early in the year, the family expanded their household by taking in the wife's father. The father, a sixty-nine-year-old divorcée, is in good health. The only medical condition noted is high blood pressure and high cholesterol. No other chronic conditions have been identified.

In mid-August of the same year, the family expanded their household once again. The wife unexpectedly received a phone call from her aunt to go pick up her grandfather at the airport. The family, having no prior notice or timetable for the grandfather's length of stay, was just told to pick him up at the airport that morning. The grandfather, ninety-four years of age, has a heart condition, has a pacemaker, and needs assistance with basic activities for daily living.

The family gets relief from the wife's sister, who is a nurse practitioner living in the same town. The sister provides assistance by managing the father's and grandfather's medications and provides transportation assistance for their various doctor's appointments. Their mother helps out by preparing and delivering meals.

Facts about the Unpaid Family Caregiver—It Could Be You

> A typical American family caregiver is usually a woman who works and spends twenty hours a week providing care. Statistics from a 2009 survey show that 65.7 million people in the United States, or nearly 1/3 of American households (28 percent of the US population), serve as unpaid family caregivers for a family member or friend.
> Children are also drafted into the lifestyle of caring. Estimates show that 1.3 to 1.4 million children ages 8 through 18 care for an adult relative, 72 percent of whom care for a parent or grandparent[8]. (National Alliance for Caregiving [NAC] and AARP, November 2009).

---

8   National Alliance for Caregiving (NAC) and AARP, "Caregiving in the US Executive Summary," (November 2009), http://www.Caregiving.org/data/caregiving USAllAgesExecSum.pdf.

The American population is quickly aging particularly for baby boomers nearing the age of sixty-five, and this trend is expected to continue until 2030. The modern-day crisis of unpaid family caregivers for many families will be placed strictly on the shoulders of spouses and children.

Typical Family-Caregiving Facts

> - Spouses (66 percent), adult siblings, and other family members and partners all serve as unpaid family caregivers.
> - Typically, unpaid family caregivers spend four and one-half years of their lives delivering care for a family member, relative, or friend.
> - Most caregivers (86 percent) are related to the family member, and 36 percent of them care for an elderly parent.
> - Nearly one-third of American households now report that at least one person has served as an unpaid caregiver in the past year[9].

The typical unpaid family caregiver also shows some differences among ethnic groups. For example, Hispanic caregivers are typically younger than white and African American caregivers. African American caregivers are more likely to have a lower household income and/or single parent family household. Asian American caregivers are equally likely to be male or female.

Experts have noted there are some cultural and ethnic differences, which may influence expectations on families taking on caregiving roles, duties, and responsibilities. Studies show that

---

9 National Alliance for Caregiving (NAC) and AARP, "Caregiving in the US: A Focused Look at the Ethnicity of Those Caring for Someone Age 50 or Older," *Executive Summary* (November 2009), http://www.Caregiving.orfg/data/FINAL_EthnicExSum_formatted_w_toc.pdf

- Seven in ten unpaid family caregivers (73 percent) are typically employed outside the home.
- Two-thirds of family caregivers (66 percent) report that caregiving has forced them to make changes at work. Most work changes are going to work late, leaving early from work, or taking time off during the day for caregiving medical appointments.
- Statistics also show one in five (20 percent) report taking a leave of absence, 6 percent quit working altogether, and 4 percent will take an early retirement[10].

---

10 National Alliance for Caregiving (NAC) and AARP, "Caregiving in the US: A Focused Look at Those Caring for Someone Age 50 or Older," *Executive Summary* (November 2009), http://www.Caregiving.org/data/

SECTION III
The Awakening

How to Live Longer, Healthier, to Stay Independent

Eighty-five percent (85%) of adults 65 years and older want to stay in their own home . . . Many will be unable!
—AARP, 2000

CHAPTER 7

Who Will Care for You . . . When Your Children Can't or Won't

The next two decades will see the number of baby boomers needing care will swell and the availability of caregivers are most likely to dwindle . . . While 61 percent of family caregivers age 50+ also work . . . One-third of boomers may need help managing their own lives.

—Unkown

Will I Have a Life . . . Beyond Age Sixty-Five?

Baby boomers, over the next two decades, will be standing at the crossroads wondering, *Will I have an active life beyond age sixty-five?* The simple answer for many—maybe. Today we see that many seniors are living well into their eighties and nineties. Also, we see for many baby boomers that if you reach the age of sixty-five, you can expect living another twenty years trying to accomplish your bucket list of things to do.

The problem many baby boomers and young adults will face is, while caring for others like grandparents, aging parents, children returning home, and grandchildren, who will be there caring for them? Many people, especially baby boomers who make it to sixty-five and beyond, will have to reckon with at least three life-changing events that come with age as discussed earlier: preventing and managing chronic disease conditions/illnesses, maintaining cognitive health, and preventing unintentional injuries.

Today, a healthy chunk of boomers and young adults are living the trifecta—doing it all, focusing on the now and not the future. Many adults in their fifties and early sixties are still working because they have enormous personal debt or do not have enough retirement savings. Many who are retired are sandwiched serving as family care attendants for elderly parents or grandkids.

Baby boomers and young adults taking on these lifestyle social changes should take time to ask themselves, "Will this lifestyle contribute to increased stress, deteriorating health, premature death or disability?" Also, caregiving efforts may have an adverse social effect on teenagers and young adults witnessing the challenges of caring for aging parents and grandparents. The question for many young adults to ponder and research is to ask, "Will the next generation seek alternative remedies to avoid caregiving duties and responsibilities?"

Living healthy to maintain one's health and independence is the central concern for baby boomers as they enter their sixty-five-plus years. The goal for many is to travel and see the world; for others, it's maintaining independence to stay healthy and live in one's own home and community for as long as possible.

The concern for many adults, especially baby boomers, is that many people will need help in managing their aging lifestyles. Adults' hectic lifestyles, unhealthy behaviors, and life-altering events take a toll and add stress. These stressors such as suddenly caring for an aging parent(s), unexpected or unmanaged health conditions, cognitive impairments, dwindling personal finances, and adult children returning home raise concerns about the modern-day lifestyle. These concerns raise the serious question again, *"Who will care for you?"*

Today, living healthy to maintain one's independence requires careful planning. Many adults have not planned for life circumstances before fifty; nevertheless beyond sixty-five, and many may need help caring for themselves. Sandwich generations are under a tremendous amount of stress just trying to live their own lives. Maintaining one's health beyond sixty-five requires effort and a behavioral change. Working beyond sixty-five requires one to stay healthy. Caring for loved ones In addition creates more modern day challenges and responsibilities that will adversely affect one's health and physical wellbeing.

Living healthy in these modern days has also spilled over on our elected officials. Look no farther than federal and state governments' gridlocked and dwindling state resources to address senior issues. Will there be Medicare and Social Security in the future as we know it today? Will there be policy changes in long-term care? Will they allow increased restitution and payment for unskilled family caregivers in the home? Even Meals on Wheels has been hit by the budget axe for many seniors.

The Family Assessment Exercise

The following family assessment exercise, "Who Will Care for You?" is an attempt to have you take notice and understand that your children may be unable to care for you. Life presents us with many unforeseen obstacles and challenges that we have to address daily. The first obstacle is the reckoning: your children, who love you, may not be there to help you in your time of need. In addition, some adult children have medical condition(s) that may disqualify them from caring for you, and adults without children may have careers that take precedence. This is the *Reckoning — Life Uncertainties*.

Take the family assessment exercise and assess your challenges for maintaining independence as you age-in-place. Remember, family is a key central driver in helping people stay in their homes. The goal and intent of this exercise is to help you recognize the uncertainties of life's obstacles and to develop your own set of plans to age-in-place.

Family Assessment Exercise—Who Will Care for You?

Sibling Assessment (SA1)	Yes	No
Do you have a sibling to take care of you if you need someone to be an unpaid family caregiver?		
Does that sibling live far away in distance, at least two or more hours away from you?		
Is the sibling single or divorced?		
Does the sibling have children?		
Does the sibling have full-time employment?		
Does the sibling have a chronic disease condition that may make him or her unable to care for you?		
Does the sibling have his or her own special family problems—special needs child, spouse, or in-laws that will make caring for you an additional burden?		
Do you often have live-ins or frequent visitors like grandchildren that you care for?		
Do you have boomerangers—grown children who have moved back home after being away and now reside with you? (Are they jobless?)		
Your Personal Self-Assessment (PSA2)		
Have you developed aging-in-place plans to stay in your home?		
Are you aware of the seven core lifestyle components for living healthy to stay independent?		
Are you reluctant to give up your independence and have your sibling manage your lifestyle and finances?		
Do you or your spouse have a chronic disease condition(s)?		

Once you have completed the exercise, go ahead and add up your *yes* and *no* answers. Since there is no scoring method, I only ask you to self-assess the challenges you may potentially face as you approach your senior years. Developing an aging-in-place smart family plan is necessary to live and protect your independence. In parts 4 and 5 of the book, you will find key lifestyle components and steps to start formulating a smart family plan to age in place.

Score	Action Steps to Take	Solution(s)
No score (SA1)	Recognize life's uncertainties and challenges for developing plans for the future when your children won't or can't care for you.	Request and schedule a 2016 CHATS area-training workshop through your church, community organization, civic association, etc. Schedule a CHATS workshop at *www.LivingHealthyandIndependent.com/training*
No score (PSA2)	Recognize life's uncertainties and develop plans for the future when your children won't or can't care for you.	Request and schedule a 2016 CHATS area-training workshop through *www.LivingHealthyandIndependent.com/training*

The Valerie McCier Story—Who Will Be Caring for You?

Valerie McCier, fifty-seven, is an unemployed, single parent of two children. Val, as she prefers to be called, started caregiving part-time at the age of twenty-nine for her oldest son. Her son, at age fourteen, was diagnosed with muscular dystrophy. Val cared for her son for ten years before he married at twenty-four. Her son's wife couldn't handle the enormous task of caregiving after ten years, so she left him. Her son was then back home in her care.

Val's life of caregiving did not end there. Her life as an unpaid family caregiver went from part time to full time at the age of forty-four when she started caring for her mother, age sixty-four and her stepfather age eighty-two. Her mother, at that time, had a major stroke that left her eighty percent incapacitated. Life for Val at age forty-four was no longer hers to live. Life was consumed at first caring for her mother, stepfather, and son.

Val's mother often begged the family to never put her in a nursing home. As the oldest of four siblings and living in the same town, all the responsibilities fell on her and her sister. The immediate family all promised that they would help with caregiving duties, but that never happened. Her mother's family helped out for a month. After that, Val was left standing alone, caring for and managing now her mother, daughter, and grandson.

Val often anticipated living out a life enjoying her children and, grandchildren but life chose a different path. Life took yet another unexpected turn for the worst when her only daughter became chronically ill at age twenty-three after giving birth to a son in 2000.

Time took its toll emotionally, physically, and financially on Val as an unpaid family caregiver. She watched her daughter pass away fifteen years later from kidney failure. Her mother also passed away the same year from congestive heart and kidney failure.

Val McCier was able to keep her promise to her mother for eleven years. Her mother passed away in a hospital and never saw a nursing home. It appears now her periods of guilt, grief, and depression have diminished and are not as burdensome as before. She is still a caregiver, living her life and caring full-time for her son and grandson who is entering sixth grade.

Finally, Val, uninsured, has taken the time to start managing her own life. For the first time in ten years, she has taken upon herself to seek medical attention to attend to her extensive medical needs.

Life of caring has been her calling and her purpose. Life has been exhausting, but she has managed to do what she could with only the gifts and abilities given to her. Still the question remains, *"While caring for others, who will care for her?"*

Reality Factors: Children Who Won't or Can't Be There for You!

Allow me to reiterate what my oldest daughter said as she witnessed our daily challenges as family caregivers: "I'm not going through all this trouble for you guys. I'm just going to find you a good retirement home to put you guys in."

Let's take a critical look why baby boomer and generation X populations need to be concerned about their future and who will be caring for them! First, family support is a key factor if one wants to maintain independence to stay in their own home. Second, caregiving will most likely come from a close neighboring friend rather than a family member.

Below are five critical factors that may raise some concerns as to why your children may not be there to care for you in your time of need:

1. Work, Time, and Distance

Issues for an adult sibling handling his or her own immediate family, relationship, work, and caregiving are enormous. Most parents who need help won't bother to ask for help. Parents don't want to feel they're intruding in the lives of their children and often times not asking for help causes more issues and even exacerbates negative health outcomes, causing injury and disability.

Caregiving from a distance is hard and costly for the family member providing oversight as the caregiver. The cost associated with time, travel, phone calls, missed work, and increased personal out-of-pocket expenses takes a toll on everyone. Most elderly parents would rather use the practice of silence and avoidance than ask for help.

> *Solution:* Talk. Having an open discussion to help cope with the aging parent's anxieties around not asking for help may be helpful. Engage in open conversations with children about a plan or course of action. Have siblings become familiar with the Family and Medical Leave Act to help plan and manage the caregiver's emergencies. Encourage siblings to be open with their employers. The siblings' frank discussion with their employers, administrators, and supervisors about their family-caregiving duties and responsibilities will ease anxiety and may help alleviate some frustrations that come with caring for aging parents.
>
> Technology has also made it convenient for the young generation's techies to work more from home. Employers are providing more variable work schedules for employees to work from home using various telecommuting electronic devices like computers, mobile phones, fax, and other remote capabilities (web conferencing/meetings).

2. Seeking Inheritance

Using the old colloquial expression, "Keeping it real," let's face it: some siblings are just in it for the inheritance. Your health and well-being may not be their priority. Your children may look concerned and may have well intentions, but they may just be waiting to collect their inheritance.

Family members who operate out of their own interests have competing egos that will make life difficult for other family members trying to care for you. Individuals who operate in this fashion are self-centered and are more concerned about their own interests and lifestyles. They operate on or feel a sense of entitlement and are only interested in the money, car, and estate/property.

> *Solution:* Beware. Siblings looking after their inheritance often will manipulate a spouse by amplifying a sense of helplessness and emphasize that they are there to protect you. Their subtle ways often will lead them to want to take control of your finances and seek guardianship or power of attorney. Be careful of those siblings that mysteriously remove valuable papers, accounts, etc., under the excuse of keeping them in a safe place for you.
>
> Part V (chapter 16) further outlines solutions for making smart family plans to address the difficulties involving family dynamics.

3. Chronic Disease Condition/Illness

Chronic conditions such as Alzheimer's disease, heart disease, cancer, diabetes, arthritis, stroke, hypertension, lung disease, and other chronic illnesses seriously compromise the quality of life for many older adults. A disability brought on by a chronic illness will be the reason for many being unable to remain living in their own homes.

Chronic conditions can affect a person's ability to live a long life, be independent, and perform everyday activities in and around the home. The inability to perform basic daily activity functions (i.e., personal hygiene, feeding, dressing, toileting, etc.) may be too much to ask of siblings to provide care for you. Helping to care for you will be further complicated when siblings' career, time, distance, and family matters are added into the mix.

> *Solution:* Find the root cause for your illness and change. The challenge for many baby boomers and young adults is having the knowledge and understanding that living healthy is the key to life longevity and independence. Living healthy to stay independent is tied to your ability to manage three key essential areas of living: (1) managing/preventing chronic disease conditions, (2) maintaining cognitive health, and (3) preventing unintentional injury.
>
> According to the National Council on Aging (NCOA), about ninety--one percent (91%) of older adults have at least one chronic disease condition/illness, and seventy-three percent (73%) have at least two. Chronic disease conditions continue to be the leading cause of death and disability for many older adults (National Center of Health Statistics, 2007–2009).

Finally, there is an increasing number of children that may not be there for you. Children are increasingly becoming affected by their own chronic health conditions which are impacting their quality of life and life expectancy. And, according to Mark Hyman, MD. He states, *"We may be witnessing the first generation of young adults that are sicker and probably die younger than their parents"* (*Hyman Enterprise LLC, Blood Sugar Solution, 2012*).

4. Competing Siblings' Egos/Personalities

Caring for elderly parents can and will bring out the worst behaviors among some siblings. Competing egos and strong personalities will often lead to challenges and sibling conflicts. Conflicts may also arise from deep-seated resentment over a parent's past transgressions and behaviors.

Other conflicts will arise when siblings' strong personalities compete for control, attention, and affection. The negative effect of this ledger is often being aloof, distant, and abusive. Most often, discord among siblings surfaces when one is considered the favorite child. Other personalities among siblings may butt heads over the denial of a parent's medical condition, quality of care, or whether a parent should live with a sibling or institutional facility.

Finally, money matters will bring out the true nature and intent of an individual. Earlier, I mentioned a sibling seeking inheritance as a deep-seated issue and conflict. This behavior is usually based on his or her selfish interest in the short term and not on your long-term health and safety.

> *Solution:* Establish a caregiving team. You would think siblings would come together to support parents' best interest in dealing with their health and safety. This is often not the case. Competing personalities generally take on different demeanors when a parent's cognitive disabilities become evident or questioned by one sibling and not the others.
>
> You may still think a family member will look after you, but it could likely be a neighbor or friend. Planning ahead for the future can minimize competing siblings' personalities and egos. Planning ahead is establishing an advanced care or aging-in-place plan.
>
> The plan in legal circles can be spelled out in one form as an advanced healthcare directive. The directive can identify a specific family member or caregiving team to make and carry out health care decisions on your behalf. The caregiving team identified in

the directive calls upon specific family members to address and carry out your specific health wishes, interests, and decisions, including estate matters.

You can formulate a binding legal document to address your future caregiving needs. You should, however, carefully consider sibling personalities along with a friend and a professional representative to make up the team.

5. Finances

The major caregiving issue causing strife and contention among siblings is finances. Conflicts will most undoubtedly arise over caregiving issues that will engulf siblings and even cause contention between spouses and grandchildren. Family sibling conflicts will be real when money is involved and parent wishes are not clearly spelled out. Money issues and contentions will also surface with an only child, a divorced spouse, distant family members, or a significant other (new spouse or estranged).

Solution: Act. Silence *is not in your best interest.* Many family-caregiving sibling conflicts stem from actions or inactions over:

- Recognizing who will take control and when to take control
- Contention over different standards and siblings' views for or over quality of care
- Coming to grips after a diagnosis
- Coming to an agreement about cognitive decline and inability to live alone
- Where an older parent should live
- Who should pay for care
- How decisions may affect inheritance
- Issues not clearly documented in a recent will

Another point of sibling caregiving conflict may involve a personal deep-seated resentment of a parent's maltreatment or mistreatment, usually a father's doing over a childhood issue. Other siblings may not know the issue. These unresolved issues often manifest in negative attitudes and behaviors that are misconstrued by other siblings as being reclusive, uncaring, and stubborn.

6. Other Factors by Default

Finally, sibling caregiving for a parent is a complex emotional issue when brothers, sisters, or immediate family relatives are involved. Additionally, as unfair as it may seem, one sibling generally becomes the primary caregiver for an aging parent. In many families, it may be the sibling closest to the parent or the youngest child.

Usually in many families it will be the younger sibling stepping-up to take on the challenges of caregiving. Therefore the family dynamics impacting caregiving for parents are enormous. Siblings stepping up to challenges will inevitably face much family strife and contention linked to their time, money, distance, emotional frustration, and other issues.

There obviously will be trouble ahead for siblings and the parents who want to believe that a child will be there in their time of need. Even more troubling are adults with no children.

Trouble is out there for family caregivers, and we're unsure of what the distant future will bring. Trouble may come from a number of fronts such as:

- Increasing health care issues
- High medical costs
- Increasing household debt
- Sudden cognitive decline/disability
- Nonfatal accident/injury causing a disability

Formulating a Family-Caregiving Team

Here are a few tips to help you identify your caregiving team. Listed below are general personality characteristics categorized by specific population generations. Siblings/friends representing these generations all bring to the table various strengths and weaknesses that will help identify a specific person or caregiving team when developing a smart, aging-in-place family plan.

Baby Boomers: Born 1946–1964, this generation is retired or soon to be retired. They represent seventy percent (70%) of the consumer wealth and are most likely to spend money caring for or supporting parents, siblings, family members, or friends.

They are confident, independent, and self-reliant. This generation grew up in an era of wealth, prosperity, and recession. Baby boomers are critical of the younger generations' lack of work ethic and commitment to career and excellence.

This generation is not known for its patience. They have control issues and are arrogant and selfish. This side of them often results in family strife and contention. Boomers often want to direct and manage the lives of their siblings. They are astute, using the art of persuasion to influence people.

Health care has become a big issue for baby boomers. Over sixty percent (60%) of adults ages fifty to sixty-four who are working (or have a working spouse) have been diagnosed with at least one chronic health condition. Some reports also show that one-fifth of older workers and their spouses—seven million Americans—either have no health care insurance or have been uninsured at some time since age fifty.

Troubling times await many baby boomers, for their health care needs are under attack. Issues such as long-term care, viability of Society Security and Medicare, government dysfunction, dwindling senior-care public services, and governmental elder care policies are external factors politicians should address.

Additionally, internal factors that individuals can control are increasing personal health outcomes, illnesses/conditions from not making health a top priority, memory impairment, high medical costs, and dwindling personal finances. These are a few factors straining this population's ability to live healthy and independent.

Generation X: Born 1965–1979, they are independent, strong personalities also wanting to take control. They are the first generation of working mothers, usually divorced, with grown kids.

They are ethnically diverse, are better educated than baby boomers, have experienced going through a failing economy and recession in the late 1970s and early 1980s, are resourceful/self-sufficient, value freedom and responsibility, and dislike being micro-managed. They are less committed to one employer and value work, but seek a balance for life.

A health and safety-conscious group that believes in healthy living and medical breakthroughs, this generation embraces the concept of wellness and the importance of a healthy lifestyle.

Generation Xers are most likely to expand housing arrangements to accommodate an aging parent or family relative. They are most likely to embrace a lifestyle of a multigenerational household.

They embrace simple and easy or contemporary and traditional housing designs. Gadgets and technology are extremely important to this group. They will buy gadgets to make life easy.

This group is comprised of comparative shoppers looking for the best deals and buys. They are Internet-savvy shoppers frequently checking for the best deals and are savvy researchers looking for the best products, services, and information for children and aging parents.

Like the next group, some Xers are social media tech junkies and career workers looking after themselves and their best interests. Some individuals living far away or in large urban areas may or may not be there for you.

Plan ahead carefully if you think a sibling representing this generation may easily embrace primary caregiving duties and responsibilities. The members of this group are savvy shoppers/researchers, so use their skills in that capacity to help you plan.

Generation Y: Born 1980–2000, this group often called Yers, millennials, or echo boomers is a strange or misunderstood, mixed bag of people. They are open-minded and like living a casual lifestyle. They seek flexible balance with work and home life and often seek jobs with telecommuting options. They often gravitate to urban centers where job opportunities are plentiful.

Yers are computer/tech junkies or technology mavericks. They are frequent online shoppers and will use search engines for everything. Want a medical opinion or device? Have this group search it for you. They will search anything and everything. They rely heavily on the digital world and social media that many older adult generations may view as a distraction.

Generation Yers are college educated and will frequently return back home because of the stagnant economy. They are most likely to choose a career over a mate and parenthood over marriage (2010 Pew Research survey). They are often restrained people, are planners, like harmony and agreement, and will often go to great lengths to avoid or minimize conflict and dissension.

They are excellent researchers and will question authority when pushed or will restrain from making comments.

Gen Yers may or may not embrace a multigenerational household but will undoubtedly live in a multigenerational household. They are not worried about aging-in-place yet. However, they are expected to return the favor, having their parents live with them at some time in the distant future.

Parents should consider a sibling from this generation group to makeup a caregiving team. They are Internet-savvy research shoppers and are accustomed to finding and getting good deals via the Internet. This population group will utilize their vast network of social media contacts to obtain information and opinions on your behalf.

Friend or professional representative: A family friend or professional representative, should be appointed on the caregiving team. This person should serve as a mediator. The mediator, not the leader of the team, should be a person to resolve caregiving disputes among siblings. A mediator should be a reliable family friend or professional with interpersonal skills to keep people on track with the care plan. Tax accountants, church members, and other professionals are likely candidates to be considered.

I would encourage that the family team's representative makeup should be small, with an odd number consisting of family members or friends. Chapter 16 ("Family Dynamics") will describe in greater detail the reasoning for this action step.

Finally, caregiving is a complex emotional issue. Proactively planning for your future needs and wishes is the smart thing to do. Family matters that are not adequately addressed will create tension and conflict among siblings. This tension is usually amplified when the father dies, leaving just a spouse. Other issues may surface when the father is insistent he can care for his spouse alone with minimal assistance even if the spouse has a disability or cognitive impairment.

Chapter 8

Health Mechanisms Contributing to People Who Will Need Caregiving

Some 44 million Americans are currently caring for an aging parent, relative or friend over 50.
—NAC and AARP (2009)

The challenge for sandwich generations caught up in a lifestyle of caregiving is simply, while attending to others, who will care for them when a health illness or physical disability afflicts them? Where will they live if they are unable to live in their home? While many alternative senior housing options are available now, that may not be the case in the near future. Statistics show that eighty-five percent (85%) of older adults still want to continue living where they are in their own homes. Unfortunately, many Americans of all ages will be unable to do so. Why?

The major problem facing many Americans is reaching the age of fifty and beyond in good health. For many Americans, baby boomers and young adults will have an unenviable challenge if personal lifestyle behaviors are not practiced early in life. For many people as they start approaching their senior years, they will need caregivers looking after them!

Reaching the half-century mark, fifty is a milestone for many people, but at what cost will it impact health and lifestyle? In chapter 7, we discussed the reality— why your children can't or won't care for you. Let's now approach this topic by addressing personal health mechanisms contributing to people who will need caregiving.

The reckoning for many Americans is to become aware of the driving factors and mechanisms impacting health and aging. Factors contributing to people's forecast for ill health and future caregiving dependency involve four key life mechanisms: (1) *managing and preventing chronic disease conditions/illnesses*, (2) *preventing unintentional injuries*, (3) *maintaining cognitive health*, and (4) *eating healthy to live healthy*.

1) Managing and Preventing Chronic Disease Conditions

Chronic disease conditions such as heart disease, stroke, cancer, diabetes, arthritis, etc., are the most common, costly, and preventable illnesses of all health problems for Americans (CDC chronic disease prevention and health promotion fact sheet).

Chronic diseases are the leading cause of death and disability in the United States, as well as causing limitations in daily living activities for one out of ten Americans. Also, a CDC study in 2005 reported 133 million Americans, almost one out of every two adults, had at least one chronic disease condition (Wu Sy, Green A—Rand Health, 2000).

In general, chronic disease conditions can be managed and even prevented by instituting healthy lifestyle habits and behaviors, making health a lifelong personal priority. Evidence supports the premise that to change unhealthy lifestyle habits people must change behavior by renewing the mind. Renewing the mind is simply engaging in a new thought process and making the decision and action to change.

The inevitable outcome of an unhealthy lifestyle is this: your lifestyle will lead you down a pathway of disease, death, disability, and caregiving dependency. Listed below are personal lifestyle tips and healthy thoughts for avoiding this pathway of destruction.

A) Promote Individual Health and Wellness

Healthy outcomes can be practiced and maintained by simply renewing the mind or developing the will to eat healthy. Eating healthy is knowing when and how to eat. It's a lifestyle practice of cutting out unhealthy foods (salts, sugars, and processed foods).

Wellness, on the other hand, is an ongoing practicing lifestyle of taking responsibility for the choices we make in life. It's a lifelong individual process of maintaining a healthy balance of mind, body, and spirit.

B) Make Physical Activity and Exercise an Addiction

Making time for physical activity is one of the most important links to living healthy and better in order to maintain independence as you age. A regular physical activity and exercise program is important to both your physical and mental health.

A physical activity and exercise program will help manage most chronic diseases and disabilities that may develop with age. Weight-bearing exercises will help prevent fractured hips and crumbling bones. Certain exercises can also promote/stimulate muscle memory, like ballroom dancing, for example. This exercise has an added benefit for people to engage or stimulate social relationships, thus improving one's quality of life.

C) Avoid Risky Consumption of Substances to Enhance Recreational Experience

Cigarettes, alcohol, and drugs, including psychotropic drugs, are all substances with the sole intent of creating or enhancing recreational experience. A continuous consumption of recreational substances will lead to poor health outcomes. Here are a few facts to consider:

Smoking: Smoking is not a healthy behavior or practice. Smoking causes cancer, heart disease, stroke, and lung disease. For every person who dies from a smoking-related disease, twenty more people suffer from at least one serious illness from smoking.

Alcohol consumption: Alcohol consumption is a personal value or choice behavior. A healthy lifestyle means drinking in moderation. Although some people have a normal response to alcohol from occasional drinking, too much drinking over time changes the normal balance of chemicals in the brain.

Most studies show excessive alcohol consumption (drinking five or more drinks on occasion for men or four or more drinks on occasion for women) can lead to increased risk of health problems such as injuries, violence, liver diseases, and cancers.

Drug Consumption: Drug consumption, likewise, is a deliberate use of legal or illegal substances for medicinal or recreational use. An excessive use of drugs or other substances leads to addiction, dependency, or serious physiological injury.

Physiological injury over time may damage the kidney, liver, heart, and brain. Impairments to the brain by substances cause dysfunctional behavioral patterns, memory loss, hallucination, and even death.

2) Unintentional Fall-Related Injury

Unintentional fall-related injuries are another serious health issue that jeopardizes many older adults from living independently. Many older adults suffering from a chronic disease illness are often subject to an unintentional fall-related injury. An unintentional fall-related injury is caused from a trip, slip, or fall. A fall-related injury can significantly threaten the ability of older adults to stay in their homes.

Fall-related injuries, according to many studies, are the leading cause of injury deaths and the most common cause of injuries and hospital admissions for trauma among adults age sixty-five and older. Fall-related injuries cause significant mortality, disability, loss of independence, and early admission to nursing homes. Hip fractures and head injuries are among the most prevalent fall-related injuries that can threaten independence and increase the risk of early death.

How big is the problem? According to the Centers for Disease Control (CDC) Injury Center, each year, one in three adults age sixty-five and older fall, but less than half of them will talk to their healthcare providers about it.[11]

> Among older adults (those sixty-five and older), falls are the leading cause of injury death. They are also the most common cause of nonfatal injuries and hospital admissions for trauma.
>
> In 2010, 2.3 million nonfatal fall injuries among older adults were treated in emergency

---

11 cdc.gov/HomeandRecreational Safety/Falls

departments, and more than 662,000 (one in three) of these patients were hospitalized.[12]

Between 20 percent and 30 percent of falls cause moderate to severe injuries that reduce mobility and independence and increase the risk of premature death.[13]

Most fractures are caused by falls, and the most serious type is hip fracture (Bell et al. 2000).

Up to 20 percent of hip fracture patients die within a year from a serious fall, and those who survive often experience significant disability and reduced quality of life (Liebson et al. 2002).

Traumatic Brain and Spinal Cord Injury

Traumatic brain and spinal cord injuries are two major causes of unintentional injuries that affect people at any stage of life. Traumatic brain injury (TBI) occurs when a sudden physical assault on the head causes damage to the brain. A spinal cord injury (SCI) occurs when a traumatic event results in damage to cells in the spinal cord or severs the nerve tracts that relay signals up and down the spinal cord.

Unintentional fall-related injuries continue to be the leading cause of TBI (35.2%) for many Americans. Falls cause half (50%) of the TBIs among children zero to fourteen years of age and 61% of the TBIs among adults age sixty-five and older.

---

12 Hornbrook, M. C., Stevens, V. J., Wingfield, D. J., Hollis, J. F., Greenlick, M. R., Ory, M. G. "Preventing Falls among Community-Dwelling Older Persons: Results from a Randomized Trial." *The Gerontologist* 34, no.1 (1994): 16–23.

13 Alexander et al. 1992, Sterling et al. 2001, Wolinsky et al. 1997, Hall et al. 2000.

Older adults with fall-related injuries have the highest rates of TBI-related hospitalization and death.

> The most common causes for TBI's are falls (35.2%), motor vehicle—traffic (17.3%), struck by/against events (16.5%), and assaults (10%). Spinal cord–injury causes (SCI) are motor vehicle accidents (46%), falls (22%), violence (16%), and sports-related injuries (12%)
> (CDC.gov/HomeandrecreationalSafety/Fall/adultfalls.html).

The demographics show that most unintentional injuries happen to males (59%), and they are more often diagnosed with a TBI usually because of high-risk behavioral activity. Most SCI cases show an estimate of 50% to 70% of SCIs occurs in ages fifteen to thirty-five years of age.

Racial/ethnic breakdowns show similar distribution patterns for both TBI and SCI cases, whites making up 65% of the cases; African Americans 25%; Hispanics 8%; and others 2%, respectively.

In general, it's important to note a TBI can occur without a loss of consciousness. This is usually referred to as a mild traumatic brain injury or concussion. After a fall-related injury that involves some trauma to the head, clients should be watched carefully. Typically, clients who experience a mild concussion are more symptomatic after a day has elapsed than at two to four hours post injury.

Family caregivers should be aware of a parent falling in and around the home. Brain injury or concussion symptoms usually escalate for twenty-four to seventy-two hours after an incident. It's important that people who have suffered a brain injury get medical attention and evaluation on the day of the injury. The effects of a TBI can have both short- and long-term lifestyle consequences affecting thinking, sensation, language, and emotions.

TBI can increase the risk of epilepsy and exacerbate other conditions such as Alzheimer's disease, Parkinson's disease, and other brain disorders that become more prevalent with age. These conditions will lead to caregiving dependency.

3) Cognitive Disorders and Mental Health/Wellness Functions

Modern-day medical and technological advancements have made it possible for many people to live healthy and longer well into their nineties. Although aging is an inevitable process, certain unhealthy lifestyle choices are associated with aging, cognitive disorders, and poor mental health.

Medical advances have gracefully handed people a gift for living longer. However, while people live longer there still remains a serious lifestyle challenge with the health and physical conditions that people will continue to have in their sixties, seventies, and eighties. Who will care for you when your health, memory, and cognitive functions are impaired?

Memory and learning functions of the brain start to deteriorate for most people at the age of forty. These various impairments often are due to an unmanaged chronic disease condition(s) or are associated with an unintentional injury impacting the brain (TBI) or spinal cord system (SCI).

For many people as they age, maintaining cognitive health functions is a key driving factor for performing both basic and instrumental activities of daily living. Maintaining cognitive health functions to remain independent to stay in your home and community is key.

Evidence now shows people's cognitive disabilities are starting early in life and are not just relegated to increased age. Although functional impairment does increase with age, living healthy with mind and memory intact will reap great senior rewards of staying active, healthy, happy, and independent.

> Cognitive disorders are usually associated with medical terms such as Alzheimer's disease, Parkinson's disease, chronic brain disorder, mood disorders like sundowning, and others. Dementia is a condition in which a normal function of the brain progressively deteriorates over time, resulting in memory loss and confusion. Amnesia is often brought about by head trauma.

An aging parent's deteriorating cognitive impairment forces many family members to quickly consider a senior-care facility for parents. A lack of understanding of the true cause and nurture of the cognitive disorder can cause irreversible harm and hardship to an elderly parent. Note, a parent may perceive he or she is being pushed away.

It's important to note that cognitive disorders can often be triggered by a number of different factors. A quick rush to judgment of some family members to institutionalize someone is not always the best course of action until all options are explored. Here are a few factors for families to consider:

- Certain medications
- Drug toxicity causing lack of oxygen to the brain (delirium)
- Brain infections (meningitis or encephalitis)
- Head trauma (TBI/MTBI)
- Alcohol dependency
- Severe vitamin deficiency
- Tumors, surgery, strokes, or brain inflammation (hypoxia)

Many adults will experience some deterioration in cognitive functions affecting memory, ability to learn new technology, speed of processing information, language, speech, and other mental functions. These cognitive impairments can be managed with proper medical attention.

Many people who are lucky to have family-caregiver support should be commended for their tireless efforts. According to the Alzheimer's Association, there are over *fifteen million Americans providing unpaid care services for persons with Alzheimer's or other dementias*. Other facts are the following:

- About eighty percent (80%) of care is provided at home and is delivered by an unpaid family member or friend.
- At least eight hundred thousand Americans with Alzheimer's disease and other forms of dementias live alone.
- One in eight older Americans has Alzheimer's disease, and more than five million Americans are living with Alzheimer's disease.
- Alzheimer's disease is the sixth leading cause of death in the United States and the only cause of death among the top ten in the United States that cannot be prevented, cured, or even slowed.

Why are unpaid family caregivers not compensated for their time and efforts as health care attendants?

4) Eating Healthy to Live Healthy

Chapter 12, Module Component #3 is an important lesson module directing people's attention to making health by eating healthy a top lifestyle priority. This important lesson is a key mechanism contributing directly to a pathway of health, life and longevity.

Living a healthy lifestyle starts early in life when people's eating habits, choices and decisions, are embraced and practiced early in life. The consequences for not practicing a healthy lifestyle whereby what we eat has to be the top priority will only cause problems as we age. Stay tuned and read on, we have just touched the surface of this modern day reckoning crisis.

CHAPTER 9

Understanding the Necessity for Formulating an Early, Smart Family Plan to Age-in-Place

Lifestyle stressors are often exacerbated by our work culture, therefore . . . ***"Do you work to live or live to work."***
—Unknown

Chronic Lifestyle Stressors Impacting Health, Aging, and Independence to Age-in-Place

The day of reckoning for many Americans will come in one of two forms: those who will eventually be caregivers and those who will need caregiving. This chapter is intended to promote awareness for all individuals, regardless of age, to begin formulating an early smart family plan to age-in-place.

Why the fuss? An awareness was introduced early in the book, *The Reckoning*. People need to become aware of the connection of a healthy lifestyle and chronic life stressors that affect one's quality of life for living healthy and staying independent.

The pathway for living a healthy, quality life to age gracefully in our own homes and communities has been predestined and set in motion by (1) our parents' health and wellness decisions bestowed on us as children and (2) how we, as young adults, manage modern-day lifestyle challenges.

The harsh reality for many people is that a healthy lifestyle and managing various life crises is key to one's overall health, wellness, and longevity. Practicing healthy lifestyle habits in this modern-day era is, at best, difficult to sustain yet maintain. Therefore, the future holds one true fact, as people grow old, there will be a need for caregivers and caregiving.

Previously, in chapter 3, both intrinsic and extrinsic lifestyle factors impacting quality of life and caregiving dependency were mentioned. Listed there were key determinants affecting quality of life and how people manage their everyday chronic lifestyle stressors. It's these lifestyle stressors that are threats to overall health and wellness that will eventually, wreak havoc on the mind and body, causing disease, disability, and early death.

The arduous challenge for many people managing these chronic life stressors is becoming aware of both the internal and external challenges and decisions that culminate in either a healthy or unhealthy lifestyle.

A chronic lifestyle stressor is a condition that places a demand on the body's physical, mental, and emotional energy. Over time, as people age, these life stressors eventually become habit-forming and a lifestyle that triggers health problems.

A constant and continuous level of chronic stress has damaging consequences for our health and body. Chronic stress can cause anxiety disorders, depression, diabetes, digestive problems, heart diseases, high blood pressure, sleep disorders, and more.

Lifestyle stressors are often exacerbated by work culture ("Do you work to live or live to work?"). Other external life stressors include seeking and maintaining employment, transportation expenses, managing parents' household and accounts, cultivating or maintaining personal relationships, time allocation attending to needs of children/grandchildren, juggling finances, carrying on with basic human necessities of life and more. All these life stressors, over time, take a toll.

Health and wellness come with a huge price tag and personal commitment. The toll the body encounters will affect the individual's ability to live and maintain a better quality of life as he or she grows older. The toll the body encounters leads to disease, disability, death, and family discourse. It's these life stressors brought on by risky behaviors, emotional decisions, corporate industry greed, and governmental and environmental factors that are the root problems and pathways to adverse health outcomes, caregiving dependency, institutionalization, or early death.

The Necessity for Aging-in-Place Planning

Understanding the necessity for formulating an aging-in-place family plan is the key to living in your home safely and independently as you age. It's important to be proactive by planning ahead for the enviable medical emergencies like when an injury or medical condition curtails or takes away independence and quality of life.

Being ill-prepared for life's medical incidences will come—it's inevitable. Surviving a medical incident with health, mind, and memory intact does not always happen without challenges (heart attack or stroke). Having an aging-in-place plan that outlines your family's in-home, long-term, life-care instructions is your personal assurance and peace of mind for staying in your home.

First, the term aging-in-place as previously mentioned, is a movement. It's a term used to describe a person's desire to live in his or her own home and community for as long as possible.

Aging-in-place does not fix an already-existing problem. Aging is a human process that takes place over a time. The focus of aging-in-place is helping ensure loved ones can live where they are for as long as they can.

Aging-in-place planning is a proactive planning process that documents, coordinates, and facilitates services, including caregiving support needed to maintain a comfortable quality of life environment for self and loved one(s). The importance of an aging-in-place plan is to create a lifestyle-action strategy for living and staying healthy.

The strategic purpose of the planning process is to focus on details for maintaining a lifelong, quality lifestyle regimen covering health and wellness, physical activity, home-safety modifications, short or long-term family finances; personal, legal, and life-care services; family-caregiving responsibilities; and more.

Adults are aware that adverse health outcomes and medical emergencies will happen at any time and at any age. Being prepared by having a smart, aging-in-place family plan is the key to maintaining a quality lifestyle that will pay huge health rewards with age.

Also, formulating an aging-in-place, smart family plan is a first step toward avoiding family conflict and contention. It's especially helpful for a significant other and children when a spouse dies early. The plan spells out life-care action strategies that may or may not be included in a will.

Formulating an aging-in-place plan is essential so that the spouse, family members, and siblings are aware of your in-home, long-term, life-care wishes involving:

- Where you want to go if you can no longer reside in your home;

- How you want to be taken care of;
- What steps, duties, and responsibilities certain family members or relatives need to assume as unpaid family caregivers and more.

These are a few life-care issues that will be addressed in more details in the following sections, parts 4 and 5.

Aging-in-place planning is a strategic, in-home family plan of life-care instructions. Like household financial plans, college plans for children, vacation plans, or family emergency preparedness plans, it is an important life-care step to protect you and your family's needs.

Introduction to Key Core Lifestyle Components for Living Healthy and Aging-in-Place Planning

An aging-in-place plan provides peace of mind and security for self and loved ones to maintain an optimum level of health and independence to stay in their home. The plan is a strategic, life-care family document that outlines key core family lifestyle components for living healthy to age-in-place. The intent of the document is to minimize family conflicts over finances, inheritance, and end-of-life wishes. In addition, the document lists location(s) and which family member to reside with if unable to live in one's own home.

A smart, aging-in-place plan assures that future caregiving arrangements are planned in advance to maintain quality of life when health, safety, and independence are questioned. The plan, at a minimum, should address key areas such as home care and homemaker/aide/attendant service needs. In addition, medical management and medication monitoring, transportation, and safety (legal, financial, in-home security, and more) should be addressed.

Understanding the need to formulate a smart, in-home, life-care family plan is a key step in protecting your personal wishes for staying where you are, in your own home. Taking responsibility early in life as a young adult to live healthy will ensure staying healthy and independent as you age.

There are seven core fundamental lifestyle components for formulating a smart family plan to age-in-place. These multifaceted lifestyle and caregiving principles are your guide for living healthy and better to maintain independence.

Sections IV and V will begin to outline the challenges in taking control of the future. The necessary first step for you to take is to start formulating your own in-home, long-term-care, smart family plan for living healthy to age-in-place. These two sections will spell out completely both intrinsic and extrinsic lifestyle components to keep people living healthy and independent staying in your home.

These are key foundation components for formulating smart plans for living healthy and better to maintain independence. The multifaceted approach as outlined will address vital living-healthy and caregiving components in order to take corrective action for loved ones to age-in-place. The goal is to ensure future livability by focusing on health, wellness, safety, and caregiving support to maintain independence as you gracefully age.

The seven key core family lifestyle components for living healthy to age-in-place begin here as your individual lifestyle lesson guide. These components will help you develop and formulate your own in-home, long-term, aging-in-place plan. The seven key steps for securing your future independence will focus on the following:

> Step 1: Understanding the Synergistic Effects of Chronic Disease Conditions on Aging

Step 2: Physical Activity and Exercise—to Stay Healthy and Independent

Step 3: Eating Healthy to Live Healthy

Step 4: Environmental Home Modifications—Health and Safety Strategies for Staying in Your Home

Step 5: In-Home Long-term Care Planning

Step 6: Legal and Life Care Planning—Elder Care Issues and Documents

Step 7: Family Dynamics of Caregiving

The reckoning is here affecting everyone at every stage of life regardless of age. Most assuredly, someday in the not-so-distant future, you will need a family member to care for you. Will there be someone for you?

SECTION IV
The Intervention (Part I)

Intrinsic Components #1 through #4

Key Components for Formulating a Smart Family Plan to Age-in-Place

> Aging-in-Place is the ability to live in one's own home and community safely, independently and comfortably, regardless of age, income or ability level
> *Centers for Disease Control*
> *Healthy Homes - Terminology*

CHAPTER 10

Module Component #1
Understanding the Synergistic Effects of Chronic Disease Conditions on Health and Aging

Chronic Disease conditions causing illness, death and disability can be prevented . . . Unfortunately 1 out of every 2 adults, have at least one chronic disease condition.
—Centers for Disease Control 2005 Study

The State of Health and Aging

Chronic disease conditions are characterized by a complex combination of multiple risk factors that are both behavioral and environmental. Mentioned in the previous chapter were three lifestyle behaviors people must address to live healthy. They are (1) promoting individual health and wellness, (2) making physical activity and exercise an addiction and (3) avoiding risky consumption of drugs and alcohol, including smoking/tobacco use.

In this chapter is a critical look at the synergistic effects of chronic disease conditions on health and lifestyle. Here the term synergistic is used, showing the total working effects of chronic disease conditions on lifestyle, eating habits, and environment which affect health and aging.

Chronic disease conditions causes many illnesses: Alzheimer's/dementia, heart disease, cancer, diabetes, arthritis, stroke, lung disease, and many others. These unhealthy conditions seriously compromise quality of life. In 2013, the Centers for Disease Control (CDC) listed *obesity* as a chronic condition.

Chronic disease conditions are the most common, costly, and preventable health illnesses affecting all people at every age in life. A CDC 2005 study shows the following:

- One out of every two adults has at least one chronic disease condition.
- By age eighty, people will have at least three chronic conditions while taking five or more medications.
- Chronic conditions are the leading cause of illness, death, and disability but most importantly will seriously compromise the quality of life.

Chronic illnesses place a tremendous burden on a spouse and family members who have to care for someone with a disability from a chronic disease condition. The challenge for all generations is to make health a top priority. The end game is to (1) gracefully age-in-place by instituting early a healthy lifestyle and (2) prevent or manage chronic illnesses that negatively impact quality of life.

The stakes are high for many sandwich generations, because people have not taken seriously what it would take to live and stay healthy to age-in-place. Chronic disease illnesses have been increasing for all people at every stage of life. Baby boomers and future generations must now consider how to make it to age sixty-five and beyond with health, mind, and memory intact.

Another health and aging factor to consider is women will outlive men. That gap however has been closing rapidly as more women take on greater life stressors like managing businesses/people and relationships, smoking/drinking, working long hours, traveling, and raising children. These lifestyle challenges will exacerbate a chronic disease condition.

Longevity is not promised to everyone, especially in this modern-day era. Accidents and injuries will occur, and disease, death, and disability are inevitable outcomes. Men will most likely die early from their diseases, while women will most likely be caregivers managing loved ones with disabilities. Life doesn't necessarily mean a healthier life, but a chronic disease condition should be considered a warning sign or pathway to disease, disability, and destruction.

Generations should not take nonchalantly the importance of health and wellness in these modern days. People should not have to succumb to chronic illnesses early in life. Living healthy is knowledge in knowing how our genes, lifestyle, and environment impact our health and behavior. The questions to consider: Can I change? Do I want to change?

The Real Harsh Reality—Living Healthy Is a Lifelong Lifestyle Behavior

The real health challenge for many people is that chronic disease conditions can be prevented. The harsh reality for many people is reflected in lifestyle actions and habits. People's modern-day lifestyle behavior may never change. Why is this a fact? A quote by journalist Rula Jebreal, sums people up nicely:

> "Americans are the most entertained people in the world and are also the most ill-informed people".

Here lies the number one health challenge facing many Americans: exercising the will and wisdom to live healthy. Living healthy takes on a lifestyle behavior change. A healthy lifestyle behavior change requires people to renew the mind by changing values, emotions, actions, and habits. A healthy lifestyle should, therefore, be a daily obsession or lifestyle addiction.

A healthy lifestyle is a lifelong practicing behavior. The outcome measure is to make health a personal lifestyle priority. The benefit of this lifestyle is to keep health, mind, body, and memories intact.

One could give in to the temptation and provide an excuse that people's apathy and lack of awareness to establish new health values are at the crux of the matter. That would be a simple and easy explanation. However, the Internet, social media, and food-packaging labels provide a ton of information to keep us aware of healthy choices. Health insurance providers, in addition, are also focusing greater resources toward health and wellness.

What's the problem, people? Why do people not take heed of the health crisis that is leading to a pathway of disease, disability, and caregiving dependency? I'll begin by offering a simple life prescription. "Do what's right. Then do the things that are right." This will change your life.

Doing what's right is the state or ability of having knowledge (awareness). Doing the things that are right is a practice of implementing personal decisions to institute corresponding actions and habits to change behavior. Therefore, the aging-in-place lifestyle health lesson to take away is as follows:

<u>Aging-in-Place Lifestyle Lesson Nugget #1:</u>
You will never change your life until you
commit to changing your routine.

Mechanisms Contributing to Chronic Disease Conditions: The Epidemic Crisis

This section will be an attempt to outline some of the real health crises impacting chronic disease conditions. This section will quote some statistics about specific chronic disease conditions and will also provide a glimpse at various mechanisms (factors) contributing to the crises. Below are six epidemic crises that are at the forefront of increased incidence of chronic illness and unhealthy outcomes.

First, three key areas categorize mechanisms contributing to the chronic disease epidemic are: personal factors, big-business/food industry, government policies and environmental factors. Let's carefully look at these contributing factors that are at the root of the epidemic. Personal decisions and unhealthy behaviors contributing to the chronic disease epidemic are things you can change. In addition to behaviors you can institute are two other external factors contributing to the epidemic. These other factors will be discussed in chapter 12, "Eating Healthy to Live Healthy."

- Personal factors (determinates)
    - Obesity/overweight
    - Prediabetes/diabetes
    - Smoking/tobacco use and alcohol consumption

- Big-business/food industry and government
    - Modern drugs and antibiotics
    - Chemicals in food supply

- Environment
    - Contaminants from industry pollution

Aging-in-Place Lifestyle Lesson Nugget #2:
Be informed, for you cannot take for granted that someone is looking out for you!

---

1. Obesity/Overweight: Epidemic Crisis (One of Six)

Obesity, over the last two decades, has been a major health issue for Americans. Obesity was recently classified as a chronic disease condition by the Centers for Disease Control and Prevention (CDC). CDC reported in 2010 that one in three adults (35.7 percent) and one in five (17 percent) American children are obese (CDC, NCHS 2010 national obesity trends).

The health effects of obesity, including being overweight, is a gateway trigger leading to a variety of chronic illnesses like arthritis, hypertension (high blood pressure), diabetes (type 2), heart disease, liver/gallbladder disease, osteoarthritis, stroke, sleep apnea, gynecologic problems, and others. Obesity not only impacts lifestyle, but it can also lead to lower self-esteem, depression, discomfort in social situations, and a significantly diminished quality of life.

Obesity is generally defined as an excessive amount of body fat. Obesity, in numeric terms, refers to a body weight that is at least thirty percent over the ideal weight for a specified height. More commonly, obesity refers to any individual with a body mass index (BMI) of more than thirty (30). A BMI of 18.5 to 24.9 is considered healthy; 25 to 29.9 is overweight.

According to the National Institutes of Health (NIH), the term overweight refers to body weight that is at least ten percent (10) over the recommended weight for a certain individual's weight and height class. Overweight, in common terms, refers to an individual with a BMI of more than twenty-five (25).

Obesity Facts

More than one-third of the US general adult population (35.7 percent) is obese, and seventeen (17) percent of youth is obese (data from the National Health and Nutrition Examination Survey 2009–2010).[14]

Obesity often is the leading cause of preventable death in the United States. Some studies show gaining eleven to sixteen pounds doubled the risk of type 2 diabetes, while gaining seventeen to twenty-four pounds tripled the risk (*Hyman Enterprise LLC 2012*).

Obesity Racial/Ethnic Disparities

> Non-Hispanic blacks have the highest age-adjusted rates of obesity (49.5 percent) compared with Mexican Americans (40.4 percent), all Hispanics (39.1 percent), and non-Hispanic whites (34.3 percent).[15]

Obesity and Socioeconomic Status

- Among black non-Hispanic and Mexican American men, those with higher incomes are more likely to be obese than those with low incomes.
- Higher-income women are less likely to be obese than low-income women.
- There is no significant relationship between obesity and education among men.
- Among women, there is a trend—those with college degrees are less likely to be obese compared with less educated women.
- Between 1988–1994 and 2007–2008, the prevalence of obesity increased in adults at all income and education levels.

---

14 The National Health and Nutrition Examination Survey 2009–2010
15 Obesity data from the National Health and Nutrition Examination Survey 2009–2010

Obesity and Children

Today, because of a sedentary lifestyle, poor nutritional habits, and chronic health conditions, we're raising the first generation of young people who may live sicker and die younger than their parents.[16]

Here are some statistics about children to ponder:

- One in three children are overweight in America.
- Childhood obesity has tripled from 1980 to 2010.
- One in three children born today will have diabetes in their lifetime.

2. Diabetes/Prediabetes: Epidemic Crisis (Two of Six)

Diabetes strikes people of all ages and all races, and early symptoms for diabetes are subtle. Diabetes thwarts the body's ability to use carbohydrates in food for energy. The result is elevated blood sugar. Over time, this excess sugar raises the risk for heart disease and stroke, hypertension, loss of vision, kidney disease, nerve and organ damage, and other serious chronic conditions.

> Diabetes starts when the body's pancreas does not produce enough insulin. Insulin helps turn food into energy. The stomach breaks down carbohydrates from food into sugar or glucose. Glucose then enters the bloodstream, which stimulates the pancreas to release insulin, a body hormone. Insulin allows glucose to enter cells throughout the body, where it is used as fuel. Excess glucose is stored in the liver.

---

16 Hyman M., Hyman Enterprise LLC, The Blood Sugar Solution, February 2012

The prevalence of diabetes in the United States has tripled since the 1980s. Facts on diabetes from the CDC National Diabetes fact sheet (national estimates and general information on diabetes and prediabetes in the United States) show the following:

- In 2010, 25.8 million Americans, or one out of three people had diabetes.
- Reports also show some 18.8 million people have been diagnosed with diabetes by a healthcare professional.
- Some 7.0 million people are undiagnosed.

Diabetes is the seventh leading cause of death for people of all ages in the United States. Statistics show for age group twenty-five to fifty, it's the eighth leading cause of death, and for age group fifty to eighty-five, it's the seventh leading cause of death.

Diabetes is a major cause of heart disease and stroke for all people in the United States. For people of age group twenty-five to eighty-five, heart disease ranks number one as the leading cause of death indicator. Stroke is the third leading cause of death indicator for the same age group. Diabetes is also the leading cause of kidney failure, non-traumatic lower-limb amputations, and new cases of blindness among adults in the United States.

Prediabetes is a state in which some but not all, diagnostic criteria for diabetes are met. It is often described as the gray area between normal blood sugar and diabetic levels.

Prediabetes is a subtle indicator that the body is showing signs of insulin resistance or insulin deficiency. Insulin resistance (IR) is a physiological condition in which cells fail to respond to the normal actions of the hormone insulin.

Based on national estimates from the study 2005 to 2008 on fasting glucose or hemoglobin A1c levels, prediabetes was determined to be found in the following:

- Thirty-five percent (35%) of US adults aged twenty years and older
- Fifty percent (50%) of adults aged sixty-five years and older
- Applying these percentages to the entire US population in 2010 yielded an estimated seventy-nine million American adults aged twenty years and older with prediabetes.

Women who have had gestational diabetes and pregnant women without a previous diagnosis of diabetes, develop a high blood glucose level and have a thirty-five percent (35%) to sixty percent (60%) chance of developing diabetes in their latter years (within ten to twenty years). Currently, reported rates of gestational diabetes range from two percent (22%) to ten percent (10%) of pregnant women. Immediately after pregnancy, five percent (5%) to ten percent (10%) of women with gestational diabetes are found to have diabetes, usually type 2.[17]

Studies now show that new diagnostic criteria for gestational diabetes will increase the proportion of women diagnosed with gestational diabetes. Using the new diagnostic criteria, an international multicenter study of gestational diabetes found that eighteen percent (18%) of pregnancies are affected by gestational diabetes.

Other important diabetes risk factors are the following:

- Race and ethnicity. Hispanics, African Americans, Native Americans, and Asians have a higher than average risk for diabetes.
- Family history of diabetes. Having a parent or sibling with diabetes boosts risk.
- Age. Being forty-five and older increases risk of type 2 diabetes.

---

17 JAMA 307, no. 5 (2012): 491–497, doi: 10.1001/jama.2012.39.

- Obesity/overweight. Increases odds of developing type 2 diabetes (a BMI of 18.5 and 24.9 is considered healthy; 25 to 29.9 is overweight).
- Apathy. Not being interested or concerned about instituting healthy lifestyle behaviors and developing healthy eating habits to determine how food affects your blood sugar.

3. Smoking/Tobacco Use and Alcohol Consumption: Epidemic Crisis (Three of Six)

Smoking and tobacco use cause cancer, heart disease, stroke, and lung disease (including emphysema, bronchitis, chronic airway obstruction, and more). In the United States, tobacco use leads to disease and disability. Tobacco use is responsible for about one to five deaths annually (about 443,000 deaths per year and an estimated 49,000 of the smoke-related deaths are the result of secondhand smoke).

The Surgeon General 2014 report: "Health Consequences of Smoking—50 Years of Progress" shows significant progress has been made in adult smokers who have quit or have learned to face life without a cigarette. Congratulations to people who have quit or are contemplating quitting.

After the first Surgeon General report (1964), the new report expands and supports a new body of evidence showing chronic illnesses and other adverse health effects caused by smoking and exposure of nonsmokers to tobacco smoke. New findings show that the risk for increased adverse health effects of casual secondhand smoke is greater than previously reported. New findings from the Surgeon General 2014 report show the following:

- Liver cancer and colorectal cancer are added to the long list of cancers caused by smoking.

- Smoking increases the risk of dying from cancer and other diseases in cancer patients and survivors.
- Smoking is a cause of diabetes mellitus.
- Smoking causes an adverse effect on the body including inflammation, and it impairs immune function. Smoking is a cause of rheumatoid arthritis.

More than seventy percent (70%) of smokers want to quit. More than half of all adult smokers have quit. However, for every person who dies from a smoking-related disease, twenty more people suffer with at least one serious illness from smoking.

According to the Mayo Clinic, alcoholism is the process of becoming addicted to alcohol. Although some people have a normal response to alcohol from occasional drinking, others do not. Over time, drinking too much can change the normal balance of chemicals in your brain associated with the experience of pleasure. Most studies show excessive alcohol drinking is when men drink five or more drinks on an occasion and when women drink four or more drinks on an occasion.

According to the CDC, excessive drinking can lead to increased risk of health problems such as injuries, violence, liver diseases, and cancers. A healthy lifestyle means drinking alcohol only in moderation. Drinking on a regular basis can produce a physical dependency on alcohol. People who begin drinking at an early age are at a higher risk for a drinking problem or physical dependency on alcohol.

Family history is a genetic factor for physical dependency on alcohol. Depression and mental health problems and social and cultural environments with family and friends are also risk factors. Mixing medications with alcohol increases lifestyle dependency on alcohol. The lesson—drink in moderation.

The synergistic effects of chronic disease conditions causing illness and disability are well documented. Consequently planning to age-in-place to stay in one's own home will require life choices. Making health a top priority is a start. The process will require a change in one's lifestyle and habits that have to be cultivated early in life. Therefore, maintaining an active physical fitness routine and eating healthy to keep cognitive abilities fully intact should be the life mission for all people regardless of age.

CHAPTER 11

Module Component #2
Physical Activity and Exercise to Stay Healthy and Independent

Eighty percent (80%) of Americans do not have an exercise regimen!
—American College of Sports Medicine (2015)

Physical Activity and Exercise as a Lifestyle

Making time for physical activity is the second key step and one of the most important lifestyle behaviors for living healthier, longer, and more independently. The goal as we age is to live healthy with mind and memories intact to gracefully age-in-place. Maintaining a healthy lifestyle regimen that includes a regular physical activity as a lifestyle behavior is an important, vital component for aging gracefully.

A lifestyle that includes a regular physical activity and exercise (PA&E) regimen is the second of seven important factors for improving quality of life while aging. Starting as young adults and maintaining a regular PA&E regimen will help prevent most chronic diseases and disabilities that may develop or occur with age. Exercising will undoubtedly improve quality of life; however, finding that passion in a physical activity is a lifelong commitment along with eating healthy to live healthy (component #3).

This chapter will attempt to bring out key health, social, and physical benefits of a physical activity and exercise regimen that may help kick-start a new lifestyle behavior or habit. For others who have already embraced a fitness lifestyle, it may expand your knowledge to look at other cross-training exercise regimens. The overall goal is to focus on specific physical activities for improving strength, balance, aerobic conditioning, muscle memory, and more.

What's Physical Activity?

Physical activity and exercise (PA&E) is any continuous bodily activity that, over time, enhances or maintains an individual's overall health and wellness. Exercising is the physical activity by which physical body movements or actions are designed to attain a level of fitness or conditioning. It's a series of actions, movements, or tasks that is performed repetitiously or regularly as a practice for improving a skill, procedure, or muscle memory.

Physical activity must be a lifelong lifestyle habit, for there are great benefits for those that stay active early and often through life. Table 1 shows a physical-activity topographer lifestyle cycle from youth to adult. The table shows that from their youth, children are engaged in some form of physical activity and play. As middle-aged adults age thirty-five to sixty-five and adults sixty-five and up, people should continue embracing lifelong lifestyle fitness habits. People however seldom do for a variety of reasons.

Table 1

Risk Factors Contributing to Healthy and Unhealthy Outcomes
The Chronic Disease Condition Health Paradigm

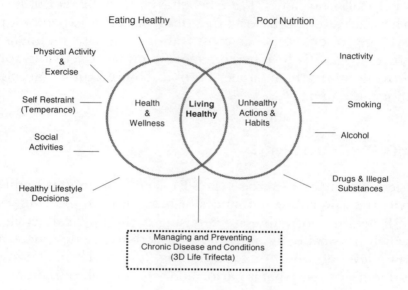

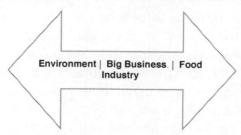

Table 2

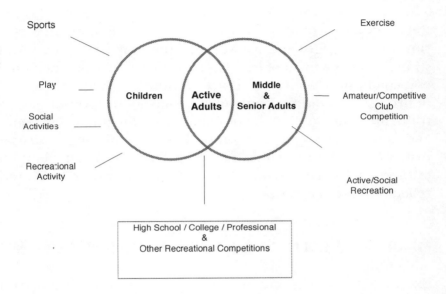

Youth, Teens, and Young Adults Physical-Activity Cycle

Sports: Informal or organized childhood associations designed to nurture mental abilities, physical fitness, and social interaction. Hundreds of sports can be classified as either team-oriented or individual competition or pleasure. Fitness activities demonstrating levels of athleticism, dexterity, and physical challenges are sports-related. This would also include musicians involved in some form of competition – for example, a marching band.

Play: Informal or organized childhood development opportunities that allow children to explore, discover, and develop cognitive skills and abilities. Playing is changing movements and actions to imitate others, exercising to stimulate fun, and playing games or acting. Play, in some professional circles, is the chief ingratiation for the development of imagination, intelligence, language, social skills, and motor functions.

Recreational activity: Leisure activity acted upon in spare time that engages the mind and body for amusement and stimulation as a form of fun. Recreational activity is a personal enjoyment of play and exercise to produce or maintain a level of fitness. Recreational activity is a continuous form of play to fulfill an individual's need or compulsion for fun, excitement, and play. Whether playing computer games, playing a musical instrument, doing gymnastics, or participating in planned outdoor activities to maintain a level of fitness, fun and relaxation are recreation.

Middle-Aged and Older Adults Physical-Activity Life Cycle

Exercise: A physical activity that is intended to keep a person healthy and fit. Exercising is bodily movements and actions designed to impact and improve aerobic conditioning, physical strength/endurance through weight training (bone/muscle strengthening), and stretching/flexibility.

Also, a well-balanced physical activity program that is both a structured and continual habit can improve one's overall mental health and endurance. Exercising for middle-aged and older adults can significantly improve balance to reduce the fear of falling.

Exercises such as tai chi, water aerobics, and other exercises are intended to increase strength, flexibility, and balance. Regular and frequent exercise is a lifestyle behavior. The outcome we all should strive for is to stay healthy and fit as we age (see exercise benefits).

Dance: A great way for people to keep their mind and body healthy. Whether it's aerobic dance training or ballroom or line dancing, they're all physical activities that studies have found beneficial for people of all ages.

Consider these physical-activity study findings:

1) Dancing may boost your memory and prevent you from developing dementia as you age (*The New England Journal of Medicine*).
2) Dancing with a partner and musical accompaniment helps bring about stress relief (*Journal of Applied Gerontology*).
3) For people with heart problems, dancing can improve heart health, breathing, and quality of life (*Italian Studies, The Journal*).[18]
4) Aerobic dance training is helpful for losing weight and increases aerobic conditioning (*Journal of Physiological Anthropology*).
5) Dancing can improve better balance in aging adults (*Journal of Aging and Physical Activity*).

The best part of dancing is that it fosters social relationships. Dance classes provide a perfect environment to meet, make friends, and hang out socially with people who have similar interests. Dancing increases your energy, fosters happiness, reduces stress, makes you prone to eat healthy, strengthens your immune system, and more.

Active living: A way of life. It's a lifestyle fitness habit embraced by adults who consider personal health and fitness a high priority. Individuals who embrace this active lifestyle try to integrate at least 30–150 minutes of physical activity into a daily or weekly routine.

---

18 italianstudies.org.uk/the-journal/

Individuals have their own individual fitness routine that works best for them. The goal is simply to be physically active, doing something every day. This can be easily achieved in many different ways by walking during your lunch hour, jogging, playing with children, bicycling, or running in a neighborhood park.

The best benefit of maintaining or sustaining an active living lifestyle is getting involved in a social recreational fitness group. Participating in a social fitness group helps sustain and supports one's continuous involvement while socializing with others. Dancing, cycling, golfing, walking, running, and any other individual or group recreational activity has its benefits for maintaining a level of personal health and fitness.

While weaving exercise into your active living routine may seem like a small lifestyle challenge, many studies have shown that even modest amounts of exercising are beneficial. A Queen's University study showed people who exercise over two and a half hours a week can live up to six years longer than their inactive counterparts! Yet 80 percent of Americans do not have an exercise regimen[19] (American College of Sports Medicine 2015).

Why do adults play the game of Russian roulette with their health? There is a clear body of evidence showing benefits for physical activity as a healthy lifestyle behavior. The goal of many is to live healthy, eat healthy, and exercise regularly to stay independent while aging.

The mission is simple: prevent disease, premature death, and disability. The long-term goal is to keep mind and memories intact while aging.

---

19 American College of Sports Medicine 2015

Cognitive and Physical Benefits of a Lifestyle of Exercising

The benefits of maintaining a regular physical activity and exercise regimen are astounding. A regular, lifelong physical activity regimen benefits people of all ages. The benefits start with training children to eat healthy, to be active, and to be physically fit. The adult benefits of maintaining a lifelong physical activity and exercise regimen are keeping health, mind, and memories intact while aging.

Personal health benefits for maintaining a steady lifestyle diet and exercising regularly are substantial. A steady regimen allows individuals to better handle emotional and mental, physical, and social aspects of life's troubles that will come with age. Here are a few lifestyle nuggets:

The Benefits of a Sustainable Physical-Activity and Exercise Regimen

1. Muscles and the cardiovascular system are strengthened.
2. A weight-loss fitness regimen for a healthy lifestyle is started/maintained.
3. Frequently regular physical exercise boosts the human immune system.
4. Regular physical exercise helps prevent chronic disease conditions and their adverse health effects (i.e., heart disease, cardiovascular disease, type 2 diabetes, obesity, and more).
5. Mental health (cognitive functions) is improved, and positive self-esteem is promoted and maintained.
6. An individual's body image makeover is facilitated.
7. Regular physical exercise helps decrease some of the effects of childhood and adult obesity.
8. Exercising regularly, at least 150 minutes per week, adds years on to life span.

Moderate and Vigorous Physical-Activity Fitness Regimen

Ideally, a physical-activity and exercise regimen has the individual engaging in some form of moderate-to-vigorous exercise activity weekly. Most experts in the field suggest that moderate physical activity should be a habit carried out every day or at least several days of the week. Vigorous physical activity should be conducted at least three days a week.

Moderate and vigorous physical activities are key for health prosperity and a healthy outcome. However, another key step is eating healthy. Eating healthy, along with exercising regularly, helps you stay active, healthy, and fit.

Let's look at moderate physical activities that should be part of your daily routine. Note: the key takeaway here is eating healthy to avoid a sedentary lifestyle.

> **Moderate Physical Activities**
> - Walk rather than ride
> - Walk during lunch hour and eat at your desk
> - Walk the dog for minutes or more
> - Take the stairs instead of the elevators
> - Do yard work
> - Play golf, bowl, dance, and more
> - Lift (curl lift) light grocery bags on the way to the car and house

Vigorous activities require an output of exercising for two or more days during the week. This type of vigorous activity is intended to improve aerobic conditioning, stretching and flexibility, muscle strength/endurance, and overall physical appearance.

According to the Centers for Disease Control and Prevention (CDC), statistics show that half (52 percent) of US adults do not meet the recommended levels of physical activity (table 2). Individuals of all ages should adhere to these recommended levels of physical activity:

> **Vigorous Activities**
>
> - Jogging/running
> - Playing a recreational sport
> - Weight training
> - Tai chi, yoga, gymnastics
> - Swimming, dancing, cycling
> - Boot/fitness camps (conducted weekly for six to eight weeks)

Adults need at least:

- Two hours and thirty minutes (one hundred fifty minutes) of moderate-intensity aerobic activity (i.e., brisk walking) every week and muscle-strengthening activities on two or more days a week that work all major muscle groups (legs, hips, back, abdomen, chest, shoulders, and arms);
- One hour and fifteen minutes (seventy-five minutes) of vigorous-intensity aerobic activity (i.e., jogging or running) every week *and* muscle-strengthening activities on two or more days a week that work all major muscle groups (legs, hips, back, abdomen, chest, shoulders, and arms);
- An equivalent mix of moderate- and vigorous-intensity aerobic activity, including muscle-strengthening activities, on two or more days a week that work all major muscle groups (legs, hips, back, abdomen, chest, shoulders, and arms).

Table 2

Approximately Half of US Adults Do Not Meet Recommended Levels of Physical Activity

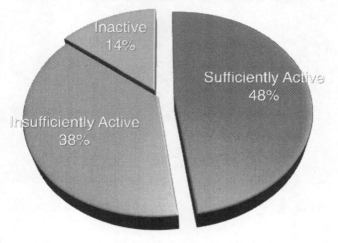

CHAPTER 12

Module Component #3
Eating Healthy to Live Healthy

"The foods you eat can be either the safest and most powerful form of medicine or the slowest form of poison".
—Ann Wigmore

Making Health a Lifestyle Priority by Eating Healthy (Nutrition)

The lesson for all to be aware of in modern days is that living healthy is the pathway to health, life, and longevity. It is not a pathway to disease, disability, and caregiving dependency. Therefore, this chapter may be the most important life lesson that I could ever teach.

Living healthy is the essential blueprint for staying healthy and independent to age-in- place. Living a healthy lifestyle starts early in childhood with breast milk as the nutritional food supply. As people age, behavior habits and choices change as lifestyle changes, and the process often takes a different pathway leading to disease, disability, and early death.

The harsh reality for adults of all generations is many will be unable to take advantage of this free life lesson that living healthy starts with eating healthy. Unfortunately, for many people, living healthy has not been a top lifestyle priority.

The challenge confronting many people today is not recognizing the impending modern-day lifestyle tsunami that is wreaking havoc on our health, lifestyle, and environment. Today, our modern-day lifestyle of living day by day or from crisis to crisis comes with a heavy price. The price tag for not making health a lifestyle priority is the reckoning crisis previously mentioned in step 1: chronic illness could negatively impact one's quality of life. A quote from Plato, an ancient Greek philosopher, says it all in one simple proverb: "Attention to health is life's greatest hindrance."

Eating to Live Healthy

The simple ingredient for living a life to stay healthy and independent is to embrace a healthy diet and exercise regimen as a lifestyle. The main ingredient of this healthy lifestyle is eating to live healthy. Eating healthy is part of an everyday practicing lifestyle or habit of living healthy. A healthy lifestyle should focus on values and how nutritional choices, eating habits, and environment will determine health outcome and longevity to age-in-place.

Eating healthy is a lifestyle that should start in childhood and continue through adulthood. The consequence for people not challenging themselves to live healthy can be expressed in a quote by Mike Adams: "Today, more than 95% of all chronic disease is caused by food choice, toxic food ingredients, nutritional deficiencies and lack of physical exercise."

Why is eating healthy so important? The simple answer is a healthy diet of fresh natural foods enjoyed in moderation is good for: preventing or managing all chronic diseases, losing weight, boosting energy, improving the immune system, and promoting overall good health. There is a strong body of evidence supporting proper nutrition as the key for managing and preventing many chronic disease conditions. Eating for pleasure, without restraints, dieting, and nutritional deficiencies pose a greater everyday risk for developing diabetes, cancer, heart disease, Alzheimer's or dementia, osteoporosis, and other chronic conditions which will increase with age.

Eating healthy is knowing how to shop for foods and understanding the nutritional benefits of foods that can be modestly and safely consumed. Otherwise, according to a research study from the National Academy of Sciences, poor nutritional habits account for sixty percent (60%) of cancer cases in women and forty percent (40%) in men.

Eating to live healthy means taking action to make health a top priority. Eating healthy starts with eating breakfast and eating at least five meals a day and exercising. Eating healthy is avoiding salts, sugars, and processed foods. These substances are the root cause of many unhealthy outcomes.

Eating healthy is embracing a daily food intake that includes grains, fruit, vegetables, milk (organic), beans, and other proteins (lean meats and fish). These are natural vitamins and minerals in foods that can boost the immune system and shield you from many common illnesses.

Modern-Day Hazards Impacting Eating to Live Healthy

In an effort to eat healthy to live healthy as we age, we must now consider other alarming developments jeopardizing our overall societal health. These societal developments are modern-day health hazards that are linked to the environment, scientific and technological advances. The end result is a potential pathway of destruction not currently foreseen and diseases resulting from a lifestyle negatively affecting our health and wellness.

Modern-day science and technology advancements have given us many conveniences to improve everyday living and quality of life. Modern-day inventions and innovations have made life easy and convenient; however, it may have also generated new challenges to address.

Recently, society has been made aware that in the process of seeking to improve quality of life and making health a top priority, another problem may have been spawned. Have technology and innovations taken us down a collision course with living healthy? Have modern-day science and technology provided a new pathway of destruction? Will greed and profit run amok over health and safety for consumers? Finally, has environmental and governmental regulation offered adequate safeguards for people to stay healthy?

The following are four modern-day developments that are threats to our ability to live healthy and threats to the environment.

1. Contamination from Industrial Pollutants to the Environment

The environment has a significant stake in our lives as science and technology collide with individuals trying to eat to live a healthy lifestyle. Look at recent news developments within the past year pertaining to air and water pollution spawned by industry or lackadaisical regulation/oversight (North Carolina, Ohio, West Virginia). Also, carcinogens derived from car emissions and industrial burning and spilling of waste into our air and water supply increase our risk for cancer. In addition, farming by large food corporations has a stake in the game, pushing pollutants and other toxic chemicals into animals and the environment.

Industry pollution to our marine life is contaminating our food supply. Increasing numbers of marine wildlife have been found to contain substantial levels of mercury. Consequently, humans ingesting such contaminated seafood are most likely at risk of methylmercury poisoning. In humans, methylmercury poisoning attacks certain regions of the brain, kidneys, lungs, and the nervous system, which could result in death (Makalinao).

2. Aquaculture Explosions and Health Risk to the Ecosystem

Big-industry fish-farming has become the fastest-growing business and should also be a serious focus of concern for consumers. The consumer demand for seafood has grown dramatically in the past decade. Therefore, is aquaculture or fish-farming the answer? At what price will it affect individual health and the ecosystem?

Table I—Ecosystem Definition

> An ecosystem is a system or community group of living organisms interacting with the environment, the interconnecting or interacting parts of plants, animals, and microbes living in conjunction with air, water, and mineral soil as a system.

Currently, the seas are running out of fish. In addition, the demand for seafood and industry products for fish feeds and fish oils have pushed the ecosystem to a breaking point. Presently, over half the fish the world consumes comes from fish-farming. How has aquaculture stepped in to meet rising global demand for seafood? Have science and technology made aquaculture a big business at the expense of our health, safety, and environment? What steps are governments taking to regulate the industry globally?

Not to criticize the modern-day aquaculture or even the poultry-farming industry, but who's watching out for the consumer? The questions remain. Have we truly vetted as health issues the environmental and public health threats arising from big-business and corporation farming? Have science and technology outpaced health and safety?

Speaking not as an expert, my investigation into fish-farming raises five fundamental concerns:

- What is being done about wastes?
- Is there a potential ecosystem imbalance of farm-raised fish escaping into natural habitats?
- What about diseases and parasites from fish-farming?
- What chemicals from man-made engineered fish feeds could impact our health and safety moving forward?

For more information about this subject, look to the documentary *Fish Meat: Choose Your Farm Wisely* by Ted Caplow and featuring University of Massachusetts Amherst fish ecologist and FCF board member Andy Danylchuk. This documentary exposes some pitfalls of modern aquaculture and the plight of the world's wild fish stocks. This documentary will help you think more holistically about where our food comes from, the food industry, and what effects new innovations will have on health, wellness, and the ecosystem.

3. Chemical Contaminants Impacting Our Ability to Eat to Live Healthy

Affecting everyone's ability to eat and live healthy are some five hundred hazardous chemicals and food additives in the food supply. These chemicals, according to the literature, have wide-ranging health effects on the immune system, reproductive system, nervous system, and endocrine system.

Modern food-production methods have opened avenues to increased exposure to environmental carcinogens and endocrine-disrupting compounds that affect overall ability to eat and live healthy. Drug chemicals, additives, preservatives, and artificial sweeteners are all part of a food industry landscape that our ancestors did not have to contend with.

Today, consumers must now contend with exposure to numerous food chemical substances as people try to live healthy. Consumers must now consider: the amount of pesticides sprayed on crops and its long-term health effects; antibiotics and man-made chemicals as animal feeds prominently used in the poultry industry; and growth hormones given to cattle and other animals, all exposes consumers to contaminants. These industry contaminants, once consumed, increase people's risk for potential cancers.

Investigating environmental concerns affecting the food supply reveals arsenic levels in apple juice, which was first brought to our attention by Dr. Oz. This created a huge stir for new mothers interested in protecting their children. The investigation into arsenic levels in apple and grape juice samples showed levels above the drinking water standard of ten parts per billion. Researchers have also found that levels of arsenic are higher in those who frequently eat rice (KwikMed in Health News—December 2011).

Scientists have known for decades that the earth's crust is an abundant natural source of arsenic. Literature reveals more than two hundred different minerals found in rock, soil, water, and air. Fumes from the burning of arsenic-containing coals and oils may cause toxicity as well. Furthermore, arsenic levels in humans can be toxic, causing impaired kidney functions and cancer.

There are many chemicals in foods people are ingesting every day. The extent of toxic and man-made, genetically-modified organisms in foods is a mystery to the average consumer. As previously mentioned, there are so many chemicals in modern food-production methods, it's hard to keep track of them all. Some chemicals improve shelf life of products, especially fruits and vegetables. Other chemicals enhance the visual appearance, making produce more colorful to the consumer.

The overall goal of the massive food-production industry is to reduce food-production cost; therefore, increasing industry profits. Consumers, on the other hand, must be constantly educated about what foods are good and bad for them. Eating healthy to maintain health and wellness and be free of a disability caused by a chronic disease condition is the safest and most powerful individual action to ensure a quality of life to age gracefully in place. Here is a quote worth repeating again by Ann Wigmore:

> "The foods you eat can be either the safest and most powerful form of medicine or the slowest form of poison."

Social media can play an important role in educating people about foods to avoid to stay healthy. While government bureaucracy and other consumer watchdog agencies take their time to research these issues, people can take proactive measures by monitoring what food chemicals other countries are banning.

Below are governmental protections and watchdog-agency terms/findings that consumers should be cautious of in their shopping or research:

- Approved and generally recognized as a safe food additive.
- The human health risk is low and not unreasonable.
- If consumed at low levels, is considered safe.
- Safe at the levels used and not a carcinogen.
- Needs to be studied further.
- Reasonably anticipated to be a human carcinogen.

Consumers, in addition, should also be extremely cautious about product-label warnings such as:

1) As long as you're not allergic, you're safe.
2) Caution: it may be hazardous to your health (1966–1970).
3) Warning: quitting now greatly reduces serious risk to your health (1985+).
4) Excess consumption of this product contributes to obesity.
5) This food may contain peanuts or tree-nut products.
6) Allergies: contains eggs, gluten, and milk.

The American consumer, through a social media consumer clearinghouse outlet, must become aware of all possible hazardous chemicals and food additives that impact people's ability to eat and live healthy. Consumers generally recognize reputable watchdog agencies looking out for the health of the public. However, these watchdog agencies have been remise, taking quick action to protect consumers while exercising temperance dealing with food-industry giants.

There are many reasons governments have been absent or failed to act quickly in informing the public of possible toxic food chemicals, while other foreign governments have acted quickly to ban questionable substances. Generally, most chemical food additives are safe, but a few chemicals, usually those with long, hard-to-pronounce names, should be avoided.

Let's look at a few chemicals that have raised concerns for eating to live healthy. This list is just a small sample of chemicals and food additives generally recognized among experts as being harmful.

- **Azodicarbonamide**

    Azodicarbonamide is a controversial chemical found in bread. The chemical is used for strengthening dough.

Subway, the fast-food chain, recently announced that it would be removing the controversial chemical from its bread. This chemical is also found in yoga mats and shoe soles and according to the Centers for Science in the Public Interest, has a by-product that is a recognized carcinogen.

- **Sodium Nitrite Into Nitrosamines**

Sodium nitrite is most often used in the preservation and coloring of food products such as bacon, ham, hot dogs, lunch meat, and smoked fish. These products, without this additive, would have meats that look gray instead of red. Sodium nitrite is found naturally in many vegetables, including lettuce, beets, celery, radishes, and others. The nitrite, however, comes with ascorbic acid, which prevents our bodies from turning nitrite into nitrosamines. Nitrosamines, according to the Centers for Science in the Public Interest, are considered potentially carcinogenic to humans. Many food companies are adding ascorbic acid to their meat products to inhibit nitrosamine-growth formation.

- **Bisphenol A (BPA)**

Bisphenol A, also known as BPA, is a man-made, estrogen-like chemical that is found in many canned foods and clear plastic bottles. This chemical has been restricted in Canada and some US states. Reports have linked BPA to a wide range of health concerns causing reproductive problems, cancer risks, obesity, type 2 diabetes, insulin resistance, heart disease, and behavioral effects[20]. In 2009 Consumer Reports tested canned foods, including soups, juices, tuna, and green beans, and found almost all the nineteen name-brand

---

20 www.niehs.nih.gov/health/topics/agents/sya-bpa/

foods tested contained some BPA. Canned organic foods tested also had lower levels of the chemical.

Particular causation should be given to BPA in canned tomato products. Reports indicate that BPA can be particularly risky in canned tomato products because the acidity of tomatoes can leak more of the toxin into the food.

- **Tartrazine and Other Food Dyes**

Kraft Foods announced last year that it would be removing Yellow No. 5 (tartrazine) and No. 6 from certain varieties of its macaroni and cheese products. Other food dyes such as Blue 1, Green 3, Red 40, and others have been loosely linked to everything from hyperactivity in children to cancer in lab animals. According to the Centers for Science in the Public Interest, these food additives are generally found in candies, beverages, baked goods, color additives, and cosmetics.

- **Silicon Dioxide, Silica, and Calcium Silicate**

Silicon dioxide, also known as silica, is generally recognized as sand that you see at the beach. This substance is also found in food as a humidity agent that causes clumping and maintains the consistency of a variety of products. Silicon dioxide is found in salts, dry coffee creamer, dried soups, and other powdery foods. The substance is also used as an insect repellent, removing the oily film that covers an insect's body, causing them to dry out and die. The EPA concluded that the human health risk is low and not unreasonable; however, some studies show respiratory problems with high-dose exposure may cause lung cancer and cardiovascular disease.

This is just a small sample of nearly hundreds of food products found on store supermarket shelves that contain hazardous chemicals. These chemical additives affect everyone's ability to eat and live healthy. It's also important to note that food products labeled as healthy may also contain hazardous-based chemicals. For additional information, see EPA Environmental Working Group Report, February 2014, and the FDA and USDA websites also have informational links for consumers.

Eating-Healthy Governance Principles for Staying Healthy

Eating healthy is a prerequisite for living healthy. It's a simple but strategic lifestyle principle to stay healthy and independent with age. Fine tuning personal lifestyle eating habits is key to be healthy, disease-free, and independent entering the senior years. Many people will not make it to that plateau of health and independence. Many will continue to pursue unhealthy habits leading to a life of disease, disability, caregiving dependency, and early death.

Below are twenty ideas to fine tune your lifestyle habits for eating to live healthy. These healthy eating tips are personal governance principles for boosting nutrients, eating smartly with balance, and having variety and moderation while cutting excess calories. These are important tips for renewing the mind and changing behavior. The goal is to establish personal lifestyle principles that will help create a new you. These principles are your personal constitution and guidelines for renewing the mind and changing old actions, habits, and emotions for eating healthy.

This is not a complete list, but it is intended to help you get started in creating a new you. I encourage you to amend this list with your own personal tips. This is the most important of the seven-step components for living healthy and staying independent while aging.

1. <u>Eat more highly nutritious foods.</u> Examples of such foods are fresh vegetables, fruits, whole grains, and lean meats.

2. <u>Avoid salts, sugars, and processed foods.</u> This will be a difficult challenge, for salt (sodium) and sugar (glucose) are in everything. The tip is to make one day of the week a cooking day to prepare several fresh meals from scratch for the week and freeze them.

3. <u>Eat five to six meals a day.</u> Breakfast is a must to kick-start your day followed by a midmorning snack, a nutritious lunch, a mid-afternoon snack of preferably fresh veggies or fruits, and a nutritious dinner. The sixth meal, when necessary, is a small snack within a reasonable time frame.

4. <u>Eating regularly prevents the body from going into starvation mode.</u> Many people unknowingly turn on the starvation cycle of the body to store food as fat, for it's unsure where the next meal is coming from. Not eating breakfast, yo-yo dieting, and other behaviors are the biggest culprits. Eating five to six small meals a day must be a consistent lifestyle habit. Eating frequently does not allow the body to store food as fat. The body will absorb the nutrition it needs to sustain itself and discard the rest, because it's being refueled five to six times a day.

5. <u>Feed the body with joy and laughter.</u> Eating healthy is the best course of action for healing the body and soothing the mind. Control stress by maintaining your joy and peace with laughter. Stress negatively affects people in many ways that lead to rapid mental and physiological changes throughout the body. Stress, for some people, triggers the gene to eat, thus leading many to unhealthy outcomes. This behavior can be overcome by eating healthy foods to reboot the mind.

Controlling stress through eating healthy, physical activity, and exercise has its rewards on controlling weight and blood sugar imbalances. In essence, laughter keeps foods away from the lips from going to the hips.

6. <u>Portion sizes should be no bigger than a fist size.</u> First, use an eight-inch plate to parcel out your food. Each portion should be the size of just one closed fist. This will take some time to readjust your mind and stomach muscles, but within a few weeks will become second nature.

7. <u>Get educated about seafood and shellfish.</u> This will be a difficult challenge, knowing what seafood is farm-raised, frozen, and freshly caught in the wild. It's also important to learn what seafood and shellfish are being imported and which environmental pollutants to best avoid.

8. <u>Target packaged-food products with five or fewer ingredients.</u> Aim to read product labels to shy away from processed-product foods with a laundry list of ingredients. This will be hard at first; however, there are food-label apps like Fooducate that can aid you in the process.

9. <u>Snack on nutrient-rich whole foods.</u> Avoid high-calorie, processed foods as your snacks. Instead, a small snack pack of fresh veggies, nuts, and fresh fruits in place of potato chips, candies, and other processed foods will have more nutritional value.

10. <u>Look for lean cuts of meats.</u> Meats like chicken, fish, and turkey are low in carbohydrates and have little fat. Meat provides the body with an adequate protein source to prevent fatigue and weakness (iron-deficiency anemia). Meat can also be a source to control weight and prevent blood sugar spikes.

11. <u>Avoid late-night snacking.</u> This is a critical tidbit that is both age and health condition specific. People over forty who do not engage in some sort of physical-exercise routine

(exercising at least 150 minutes a week) should have their last and only snack before 7:00 p.m. People under forty who maintain a weekly physical activity and exercise regimen may cheat with a late-night snack occasionally. A suitable time to cut off snacking is at your discretion; however, the general rule of thumb is to allow a two-hour window before going to bed.

12. <u>Incorporate more fresh herbs and spices into your diet.</u> Fresh herbs and spices have significant health benefits that should be maximized by you, the chef. Find ways to incorporate fresh herbs and spices in your food. Remember fresh herbs quickly degrade with time.

    Find ways to use more fresh herbs and spices as a substitute for salt and sugar. There is no need to make drastic changes, but consider how to expand the use of these herbs and spices in your favorite foods. Consider these: ground cinnamon, chili pepper, turmeric, garlic, oregano, basil, thyme, rosemary, parsley, ginger, clove, and peppermint. Try growing your own fresh herbs to have available for special meals and holidays.

13. <u>Opt out on sodas and sugary drinks.</u> Give yourself a challenge for six months. Avoid sugary soda drinks, juices, and sports drinks. Go with good, old-fashioned water with a splash of freshly squeezed fruit juice. You may be surprised how much sugar you consume, and your frequent headaches may disappear (sugar withdrawal).

14. <u>Opt out of high-calorie coffee drinks.</u> Keep it simple, and avoid the extra calories and grams. Again, consider quitting or give yourself a six-month challenge to quit.

15. <u>Add vegetables to breakfast.</u> Place a little spinach or kale in your smoothies in the morning. Scramble eggs with leftover

veggies, or make your own veggie spread to add on your bagel or whole-grain English muffin.

16. <u>Eat more healthy fat foods high in omega-3.</u> Foods such as walnuts, flax seeds, chia seeds, salmon, and sardines are healthy foods that people are not getting enough of in their daily diets.

17. <u>Swap out processed grains for whole grains.</u> The key is to increase fiber and other vital nutrients in your diet. Choosing brown or black rice is better. Whole-grain bread, whole-wheat tortillas, farro, quinoa, and so on are all good, healthy choices to consider.

18. <u>Eat more beans and legumes.</u> Explore eating more varieties of beans and legumes like red lentils, chickpeas, pintos, black beans, and more. This source of food is healthy, cheap, nourishing, and delicious.

19. <u>Prepare/serve more fresh-veggies, homemade soups, stews, and casseroles as a family meal.</u> This is a lost art that most people have forgotten. Chopped onions, garlic, herbs, leafy greens, carrots, mushrooms, and other veggies are staples for yum-yum enjoyment. Dust off your Crock-Pot and use it. There are a variety of good dishes out there to enjoy.

20. <u>Prepare more fresh smoothies.</u> Smoothies made from scratch are a great, simple way to get the extra nutrition your body needs. Thick smoothies filled with your favorite fruit or a variety of vegetables are a wonderful option for a meal or snack. Stay away from prepackaged mixes with chemically altered ingredients. The USDA offers MyPyramid.gov for you to check amounts recommended for each food group each day for the number of calories you should be targeting.

Eating to Live Healthy – Training Forum Coming Soon
Community Healthy-Aging Training Series
(CHATS) —Workshops Training Forum

Starting in 2017 there will be scheduled targeted module area workshops addressing: Eating to Live Healthy as part of the Community Healthy-Aging Training Series (CHATS)—Living Healthy and Independent Educational Agenda. These area workshops for consumers will provide tools/tips and cooking demonstrations for eating healthy.

Workshops are presented in two distinct formats: (1) a two-hour community introductory workshops at various local locations and (2) a comprehensive, sixteen-hour regional workshop at a hotel/conference center or other designated location. Regional workshops are on a limited basis according to conference host or availability and consumer interest.

Scheduling begins in the fall of 2017, and workshops can be scheduled through the project website (currently under construction beginning the spring 2017).

Chapter 13

Module Component #4
Environmental Home-Modification Health and Safety Strategies for Staying in Your Home!

Planning to age-in-place is all about creating a continuum lifestyle family care strategy that includes a home improvement action plan for staying healthy, safe and living independent in your own home.
—Pamela K. Goldstein

Aging-in-Place Planning Ahead: Making Home Safe and Livable for All!

Let's start this chapter by asking one simple question. As a homeowner, are you planning to stay in your own home, or are you considering plans to care for a parent, grandparent or relative? Taking the necessary, aging-in-place action steps to stay in your own home comes with knowing and planning for life's challenges you will undoubtedly face as time goes by. Knowing what to do is your first aging-in-place life lesson for staying healthy, safe, and independent.

Formulating a smart, long-term, family-care strategy (plan) to age-in-place is a life lesson to be taken seriously. Reading this chapter will help you identify aging-in-place challenges and will hopefully jump-start a process for planning your future to allow you to stay in your home. This chapter lesson will (1) explore expanding living accommodations to care for aging parents or relatives, (2) assess dangerous environmental home-area hazards in and around the home that may cause a serious fall-related home injury or disability, and (3) identify four specific home-improvement design options (modifications) that will allow you and your loved ones to stay in your home (age-in-place).

Homeowners need to start planning their futures by focusing on two important lifestyle paradigms: First, you will age. Start formulating your own in-home, long-term-care family plan to age-in-place. Second, if you're contemplating caring for an elderly parent, start considering home-area improvements and specific design options to expand living accommodations.

Studies show that at least fifty percent (50%) of baby boomers are currently caring for a loved one (spouse or parent) or are contemplating caring for an older parent. The significance of this trend is family households will be expanding living accommodations to care for aging loved ones.

The goal of this lesson module is to inform you about home-area improvement options to make your home safer for everyone. Component #4 is the fourth of seven critical aging-in-place lessons to adopt. People need to be aware that an unintentional injury or disability is just an incident away. The result of a serious injury or disability means an impaired quality of life, loss of independence, and perhaps needing a caregiver service for you or a family member, relative, or friend.

Indulge yourself in this brief exercise. Take the self-assessment questionnaire to assess your readiness for staying in your home.

Simply answer the following questions with a yes or no/unk (unknown). There may be some questions you will be unable to answer at this time; however, as you continue reading this chapter, many aging-in-place challenges and solutions may become clearer to you.

Self-Assessment Questionnaire for Aging-in-Place

Assessing in-Home, Long-Term-Care, Smart Family Plans	Yes	No
Is your home safe?		
When a disability occurs, will it keep you from easily getting around in your home?		
Does your home have home-improvement design features that will allow you to maintain a better quality of life as you enter your senior years?		
Will an adult sibling be willing to care for you (in your or their home) upon a disability?		
Have you personally established a healthy-eating and physical-activity lifestyle regimen that will allow you to maintain your independence to stay in your own home?		
Is your main bathroom wheelchair accessible for taking a bath or shower?		
Are the main bathroom doorways thirty-two inches wide (clear interior width dimensions) and floor surfaces capable of handling a wheelchair?		
Are you now or are contemplating caring for an aging parent, grandparent, relative or friend?		

If you answered no/unk to the majority of the questions in this exercise, you may have unveiled a host of potential long-term care problems. These problems need your immediate action to start planning now for your future lifestyle, safety, and independence in staying in your home.

Below is a personal illustration showing the benefits of an aging-in-place plan and instituting early home-modification design plans for the home.

Aging-in-Place Planning: Expanding Living Accommodations -
My Family Personal Experience

Planning the move to Georgia, my wife and I decided that it would be best to consider our future aging-in-place family needs when looking for the next home. Both of us decided it would be best to build a custom home with universal design area features (more about universal design later in the chapter).

We began seeking professional advice from certified aging-in-place professionals, including a home designer and building contractor. Blueprints were drawn up, incorporating many home-area safety features. Included in the home plan were specific area features including a fully equipped in-law suite to care for one of our aging parents in the distant future.

One autumn evening, my wife and I attended a wedding ceremony and reception for a coworker. As we were about to leave the wedding reception my wife fell, slipping off the two bottom steps, and broke her ankle. The foot required extensive surgical repair, requiring seven pins to stabilize the ankle.

Having the foresight to plan ahead with special area features for the home made life simple to care for her during her recovery period. I was able to leave the hospital, take her home, and without worry, use a wheelchair and roll her up on the installed garage access ramp to get her in the house.

Planning ahead knowing the full benefits of universal design home-area features was an education and blessing. Especially helpful was the foresight planning of the first floor master bedroom suite, with accessible bathroom features to accommodate wheelchair access, which we anticipated needing not immediately but in the distant future.

The first floor master bathroom suite included various safety features such as a walk-in, zero-step entrance, decorative stability rails (grab bars), and shower bench seat. These features made life easy for my wife, for they allowed her to independently perform her daily living activities with dignity while recovering from her injury.

This was a real life-altering wake-up call. That incident confirmed the importance that people need to closely look at home-area modifications for aging-in-place. Looking personally at my family's future health status, we already know when my wife gets older; she will have difficulty walking with foot problems (arthritis). Thus, formulating early long-term-care family plans to age-in-place is essential for maintaining self-independence to stay at home.

Planning Ahead—Home and Safety Outlook

Health, safety, and structural home-area hazards will cause many homeowners and potential homebuyers to consider making structural home-area improvements to accommodate an aging lifestyle. For many homeowners, planning ahead is key; however, making home-modification structural improvements will most likely be determined by the following:

- The incidence of chronic health conditions and illnesses are growing, causing disabilities as people age.
- Environmental toxins may be in and around the home (gas leaks, chemicals in building materials, water and air quality).
- Home structural hazards may precipitate unintentional injury due to a slip, trip, or fall.

- The lack of basic accessible home features by the nation's housing inventory is preventing older adults with disabilities from staying in their homes.
- There are inadequate living accommodations for expanding families living in single-family households.
- The prevalence of disability and chronic disease conditions are rising with age. About seventy percent (70%) of people who reach age sixty-five will require long-term care in some form during their later years ("Housing America's Older Adults"—JCHS 2014).[21]

Table 1 below shows that safety is an important consumer factor when purchasing a home. Note, fifty-five percent (55%) of survey respondents ranked home safety higher than home price on the consumer list of concerns for purchasing a home.[22]

Table 1: Important Consumer Factors for Purchasing a Home

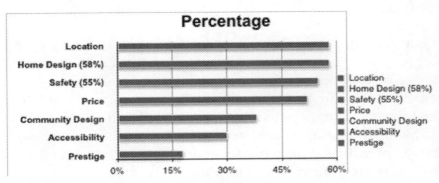

Source: John Burns Real Estate Consulting (2)
www.realestateconsulting.com/tag/consumer-insights/

---

21 www.jchs.harvard.edu/.../jchs-housing_americas_older_adults_2014.pdf
22 Consumer Insights" 2012 survey: Courtesy of Professional Builders Magazine

Housing Outlook and Challenges for Today's New-Age Generations Caring for Family

New-age generations (young baby boomers, generation X, and Yers/millennials) will be facing many lifestyle challenges pertaining to housing, health, and safety issues for today's expanding family households. Undoubtedly, expanding households with accessible, safe living accommodations for aging parent(s) will be a pressing lifestyle challenge for this generation. Why? Regionally, there will be significant housing-inventory shortages for accessible, safe housing. Homeownership rates will continue to vary widely by income and race/ethnicity, and because of budgetary cutbacks; national, state, and local assistance programs to help aging seniors will be eliminated, putting more burdens on these generations.

New-age generations, who are currently seen as distant in-home family caregivers, must now consider other aging challenges such as:

1. Aging parents are living longer than ever before, and many have various chronic health conditions and disabilities requiring care and assistance.
2. Adequate and accessible living accommodations for aging parents will require careful planning.
3. Making early home-area improvements to correct home-area health hazards for reducing trips, slips, and fall-related injuries must be a top priority.
4. Exploring the feasibility and benefits of in-home, long-term care insurance as a valuable and cost-friendly option will be important.
5. New health and home-safety technological advancement (remote patient monitoring devices) will impact new generations of homeowners.
6. Two of three older adults with chronic disabilities receive long-term, in-home care support primarily performed

by wives and adult daughters ("Housing America's Older Adults"—JCHS 2014)[23].
7. Most family caregivers report their health as excellent or very good. The longer a caregiver provides care (average of five years or more) the more he or she is likely to report his or her health as fair or poor ("Caregiving in the US"—NAC and AARP)[24].

The ideal way to address these concerns can be found by looking into the four specific housing-design trends for both existing homes and new construction. Examining these modern-day housing-design trends comes with a plethora of long-term lifestyle safety benefits.

The principal benefit for implementing early, accessible home-area improvements ensures one's ability to return home after a hospitalization and furthermore, to stay away from nursing home institutions.

Let's look at these four specific housing-design trends that the new-age generations are currently exploring:

Home-Design Trend No. 1—Multigenerational Housing: Expanding Living Accommodations

Multigenerational households are a trend that has jumped significantly in the past two decades. This industry trend designed for expanding family households is not only about grandparents and parents needing caregiving assistance in their sunset years. It's also about making financial ends meet, maintaining a better quality of life, and having personal peace of mind as the unpaid principal family caregiver.

---

23 Housing America's Older Adults"—JCHS 2014
24 NAC and AARP, *Caregiving in the US – June 2015*

Multigenerational housing is a household model in which several or more generations of families are living together, usually in a single-family household dwelling. There are many circumstances leading to multigenerational living including financial hardship, elder care matters, adult children returning home after college graduation or job loss and other reasons.

New-age generation homeowners considering multigenerational housing are leading the way and forging a new housing spurt for expanded living accommodations to care for an elderly parent, grandparent, or aging relative with a disability. The most critical social aspect of the trend is adult children are seen as therapeutic assets caring for loved ones in their sunset years.

> In 2000, the US Census Bureau counted 3.9 million American households consisting of three or more generations living together, a jump of about 60 percent over the bureau's 1990 findings.

Many homeowners are seeking expanding household accommodations and other partnership arrangements to live modestly and comfortably. The nation's housing inventory, in addition, has not kept pace with this growing social-housing trend. Moreover most homes built within the last fifty-plus years are not adequately equipped to accommodate extended family households unless major home modifications and improvements are made.

Home Modifications and Structural Improvements to Consider

Multigenerational housing is evolving and for builders, it may be more sensible to offer new-age home consumers a slew of adaptable floor plan designs offering additional features such as an elevator, a kitchenette, separate entries, and extra bedroom suites. Consumers and builders should take that note not every design plan in a community has to be multigenerational. It can just be a small percentage of a home market.

Homeowners exploring home structural improvements will be looking to make home modifications to expand living space. Homeowners looking toward remodeling to expand living-area spaces may include retrofitting a garage or basement into an in-law suite or converting recreation rooms and media centers into possible living accommodations. Those buyers considering some form of expansion should note that remodeling an existing home can be costly pending on age, floor plan, and structural design of the home.

Consumers should ask about, take note of, and further explore these four home-modification design options with several area-building contractors when discussing remodeling projects. Also, pushing the remodeling market are younger baby boomers still working, employed single adults, and divorced parents with children. These homeowners are also exploring housing-sharing arrangements to manage expenses and expanding family coming to reside (table 2).

Table 2: Home-Area Design Trends for Expanding Household Living Accommodations and Multigenerational Housing Features

- First floor master suites or dual master suite
- Master suite on all floors
- Lower-level living areas
- Living space above the garage or in an extra garage bay
- Separate entrances
- Second kitchens
- Private spaces for each generation
- Rental apartments within single-family homes
- Basement suite
- Office space
- Accessible bathrooms to accommodate wheelchair access

Home-Design Trend No. 2—Universal Design

An AARP 2000 survey revealed millions of Americans ages forty-five and older say that they want to stay in their home to age-in-place. Many aging boomers who want to age in their homes want to, at all costs, stay away from a nursing home facility. That's why most aging baby-boomers are exploring alternative lifestyle options like multigenerational or house-sharing options.

The key steps to accomplish this feat are to (1) realize the necessity of formulating early, smart family plans for aging-in-place, (2) explore the feasibility of expanding living accommodations for aging family members and relatives coming to reside in the home, and (3) make the essential home-area improvements to ensure health and safety of all family members as a top, in-home, long-term care priority.

Aging baby boomers wanting to stay in their homes may need help maintaining an independent quality lifestyle. Boomers who are considering staying put or are contemplating having aging parents reside with them need to embrace universal design as a home-modification, health and safety targeted intervention.

What is universal design? Universal design is a home industry concept that has been around since the 1970s. The goal of universal design is to ensure the personal safety for all by preventing unintentional home-related injuries.

Specifically, universal design is the practice of building or redesigning home-area environments with products and fixtures to be as usable as possible by as many people as possible. Universal design as a home-design trend and targeted intervention, targets all people (regardless of age) to help carry on and maintain basic activity functions for daily living.

A universal design feature in some professional circles is a stealth appearance that allows functionality and aesthetics to coexist. It's changing the home-design features to allow all to function independently while eliminating the appearance of an institutional facility. Universal design maximizes size and space for all to move around and the ability to reach things. Universal design allows all individuals freedom to maintain independent activity functions and also accommodates decreased mobility that comes with age and disability.

Home-modification that incorporate simple universal design are decorative lever door handles that replace traditional doorknobs. Lever door handles are easy to grasp, especially for those with arthritis. Lever faucet handles or one-touch/touchless faucets offer another upscale look and safety feature for kitchens and bathrooms.

Lights, specifically color-corrective and energy-efficient lighting should be abundant throughout the home, both inside and outside. Light fixtures with timers or motion sensors will conserve energy costs and will help people with mild cognitive impairments. Ambient lighting or LED lighting strategically placed around the home also offers health and safety benefits for reducing headaches and fall injuries.

New light switches with a rocker arm bar are also a universal design product feature. This product feature has replaced the traditional up-and-down toggle light switches and offers a wider hand-placement surface for those with arthritis. This is just one of a few simple features to consider.

Universal design is being embraced as a key and sometimes necessary home-design trend for adult generations planning to age-in-place. A recent AARP survey shows that seventy-five percent (75%) of building contractors polled by the National Association of Home Builders report an increased request for work to incorporate universal design features for homes (AARP Public Policy Institute).[25]

---

25 AARP Public Policy Institute, *Expanding Implementation of Universal Design and Visitability Features in the Housing Stock,* Fact Sheet 167, March 2010

Experts say incorporating universal design home features adds about ten to twenty percent (10–20%) to the cost of building a home from the ground up. Likewise, it is much more expensive, (depending on the age of the home), to remodel an existing home with universal design features.

Home structural-improvement projects are doable when aging parents pool together resources to offset the cost of remodeling. The cost to expand living accommodations can be justified when comparing the expense of an assisted living facility *(GA—$30,000 per year)* or full-time in-home health aides *(GA—$41,880 per year, 30 hours per week)*.

Table 3 lists a few simple universal design home-area features for those planning to age- in-place. This is not a complete list but should be considered a small sample of some area options.

Table 3: Universal Design Features for Home-Area Improvements

- Exterior front entryways with no steps
- Wider interior hallways
- First floor master suite or dual master suite on all floors
- Hardwood floors with border accents (aid individuals with poor vision)
- Walk-in showers and bench seat with decorative handrails
- High-rise comfort-height toilets
- Second kitchen
- Kitchenette/morning bar (closer to sleeping or exercise room)
- Lower-level daylight basement for an in-law suite
- Kitchen countertops and appliances strategically placed for easy access by both wheelchair users and standing persons

Home-Design Trend No. 3—Accessible Design

Accessible design is strongly related to the fundamental design concepts of universal design. Accessible design means that dwellings must meet prescribed requirements for accessible housing. Accessible design is a specific building design regulated by federal/state/local codes and standards for people with disabilities.

In the United States, the Americans with Disabilities Act of 1990 states specific public and private business and housing construction standards for what is to be considered accessible. These regulations are revised in the "2010 ADA Standards for Accessible Design."

Most accessible design features are the same as universal design home options. The differences are, universal design options have a more aesthetic look and less institutional appearance. Accessible design options may include wider hallways (wide enough for wheelchair users). There are extensive building regulations for bathroom features such as grab bars and handrails. Also, countertops can be arranged at different levels for accessible wheelchair access.

A comparison of universal design and accessible design can best be illustrated in the way you enter a home. An accessible home-design feature you'll probably see is a front entranceway with an exterior handicap ramp. A universal design home feature for a front entranceway may consist of a no-step entryway (stairless).

Home-Design Trend No. 4—Adaptable Design

Adaptable design features are practically the same as universal design features. The difference is universal design allows for function and aesthetics to coexist as decorative features. Adaptable designs are aging-in-place, preplanned design features that allow for home-area modifications to be made quickly when age or disability circumstances change.

Adaptable design means readily adjusted. It's a preplanning process for homeowners to anticipate future structural area changes as they get older. It's also knowing the enviable state of aging and health risks when an unintentional injury or chronic disease disability occurs. This design trend is especially helpful for buyers who are considering a custom-built home or constructors building community custom homes with adaptable design options.

The aging-in-place planning process allows homeowners, collaborating with builders, to formulate and develop smart home-area improvement plans for the future. Adaptable design is a home that is pre-retrofitted for eventual structural design changes. Remodeling or area modifications are then made at request when health or family circumstances change.

Examples of adaptable design features may be: the pre-installation of stacked closets from floor to floor which can be converted to install an elevator when needed; building a ceiling support structure for a bedroom retractable ceiling lift system for patients (i.e., Hoyer ceiling lift); preplanning wall-area plumbing pipes, electric wiring, and other features to install a second kitchen area. Also, electrical outlets near toilets can be retrofitted to later add comfort-height toilet with heated bidet seat.

Adaptable design features are a marketing advantage for homeowners planning to age-in-place and homeowners contemplating expanding with future family occupants. Adaptable features allow for a fully accessible dwelling to be closely refitted for future needs. These design features can be marketable to other home buyers only if the appearance does not resemble an institutional clinical setting like a nursing home facility.

Why Is Aging-in-Place Home Modification Important?

Making smart, aging-in-place home plans involve modifying areas of the home or expanding living accommodations to care for aging family members. These modern-day issues are growing concerns for all future generations. The day of reckoning will be upon you. Time and age wait for no one. What price do you place on your personal peace of mind and safety? What price will you pay to stay in your own home instead of an institutional setting?

Other studies previously cited show most people want to stay in their homes, but many will be unable to do so because of a cognitive disability, unintentional home-related injury, or chronic disease illness. Homes built twenty to fifty years ago are not adequately built or equipped with safety options to accommodate the needs of aging parents and grandparents. A home purchased and perfectly suitable at age forty may not be suitable at age seventy or eighty.

Who's Paving the Way for the Future: Homeownership, Family Caregiving, and Who Will Care for You!

The market segment of baby boomers and young adults may affect new housing construction in certain geographic areas of the United States, but in other areas of the country the home remodeling market should continue to flourish. As the job market improves young people in urban centers will seek opportunities to live in townhouse and condos while cutting car and other personal expenses. In other areas of the country south and southwest, young families will probably look for homes to accommodate their family and retiring parents leaving from the north.

Today, at least two distinct population generations are the future and principle home consumers pushing the growth and explosion of the housing market. Baby boomers and generation Xers are the main home consumers in today's market. They still have the resources to influence the market.

The growing numbers within these population groups will soon be (1) sandwiched caring for family members (parents, grandparents, and children) or (2) exploring new domestic partnership arrangements to alleviate growing debt and lifestyle expenses (house sharing). Finally, (3) the need for home-area remodeling and new multigenerational housing construction to accommodate expanding family households will spawn more business opportunities for builders, agents, and home designers.

The world's population generations are constantly adapting to unprecedented lifestyle changes. These unprecedented changes could rob us all of time, money, future earnings, dignity, and freedom to stay healthy and independent in our own homes. Finally, if you have not formulated an aging-in-place plan, then who will be caring for you?

SECTION V
The Intervention (Part II)

Extrinsic Components #5 through #7

Key Components for Formulating a Smart Family Plan to Age-in-Place

People living with one or more chronic diseases often experience diminished quality of life and loss of independence. As functional abilities—physical, mental, or both—further declines, families will need helpful caregiving tips to navigate the complex financial legal, life-care, and family health decisions for a loved one or own personal well-being.

CHAPTER 14

Module Component #5
In-Home, Long-Term Care Planning

With people living longer today . . . it greatly increases the likelihood they will develop a chronic illness requiring ongoing care.
—Jerry Stedman, CLTC, CSA
Long-term care specialist

Today more Americans than ever are raising questions about their finances and whether they have planned or saved enough to secure their financial futures. For many individuals, owning a life insurance policy and saving for retirement is the total of the planning they will do. The question individuals both young and old need to be asking is, "Who will pay the long-term care bills, which can be staggering, if I'm unable to care for myself?"

An all-too-common occurrence in long-term care planning is the tendency for individuals to believe that immediate family members will be the solution to future care needs. However, in today's transient society, adult children may live hundreds if not thousands of miles from their parents. Your adult children because of time, distance, and other restraints, may be unable to care for you.

Likewise, putting a spouse in the position of being the primary caregiver for a spouse with a chronic health illness or mild cognitive impairment will hasten the probability that not one but both spouses will become ill and need care services. The physical and emotional costs associated with the ongoing responsibilities of providing daily care for a loved one should never be overlooked.

It's true that on any given day, more than twenty million Americans act as informal caregivers either in a part-time or full-time capacity. The most proactive long-term care planning practiced by people is one in which family members react to various crisis overseeing the quality of the care that is being provided to their loved one.

Thus, time, distance, health, finances, and children's employment responsibilities all become important factors that again point to the critical question, "Who will care for you if your children can't or are unable?" Would you have to rely on friends, neighbors, and church members to assist you, or would you rather be placed in a senior-care facility?

The other critical question to ask is if long-term care insurance (LTCI), sometimes called nursing-care insurance is something to seriously consider? If staying in your home is important to you, then developing and formulating a long-term care strategy (plan) to stay and age-in-place in your own home should be part of your retirement/health care plan.

Introduction to Long-Term Care (LTC)

The term long-term care generally refers to the assistance of an individual with a chronic illness (medical condition that can be managed but not cured) or mental impairment (e.g., Alzheimer's). Assistance always entails hands-on care with the most basic of personal needs such as assistance with dressing, bathing, eating, personal hygiene, and ambulation--transferring from one location to another (*LTC Certificate Course Handbook*)[26]. Assistance can also include help with very basic housekeeping chores such as preparing meals, paying bills, or observing if daily medications are taken.

In a 1998 report issued by the US Senate Special Committee on Aging, chaired by Senator Charles Grassley (R-Iowa), long-term care is described as different from other types of health care:

> *The goal of long-term care is not to cure an illness, but to allow an individual to attain and maintain an optimal level of functioning. Long-term care encompasses a wide array of medical, social, personal, supportive and specialized housing services needed by individuals who have lost some capacity for self-care because of a chronic illness or disabling condition.*[27]

When there is a need for ongoing care, it is usually the result of an impairment that generally falls into one of three categories: acute, physical, or cognitive. Acute impairments generally result from a sudden illness or injury such as a heart attack or pneumonia. With medical care provided by a licensed hospital, the patient is expected to make a full recovery.

Acute impairments in and of themselves do not necessitate a need for long-term care. Physical impairments are generally treatable, but are deemed not curable as a chronic illness. Thus, long-term care is chiefly concerned with the daily-care needs of individuals needing chronic care, as opposed to individuals with acute-care conditions.

---

26 Corporation for Long-Term Care Certification (course handbook—October 2007. chapter 1. 25).

27 US Senate—Special Committee on Aging (1997, 1998 volume 1. report 106–229, 2000).

Unfortunately, too many Americans are experiencing the grief associated with a loved one having a cognitive impairment. Cognitive impairments include the loss of memory, orientation, and reasoning skills. It is estimated that there are more than one hundred different types of dementia.

Most people associate severe cognitive impairment with Alzheimer's. However, some individuals having a cognitive impairment (e.g., Alzheimer's or Parkinson's diseases) may still be able to navigate their activities of daily living (ADLs) and may require some level of supervision or daily assistance.

Defining Long-Term Skilled and Custodial Care

Long-term care encompasses a wide array of services that can be simplified into two categories of assistance: skilled and custodial care. For individuals who have medical conditions that require professional care provided by physicians, nurses, licensed practical nurses, or licensed therapists, the level of care needed is considered skilled. Skilled care can be provided in the home, community, or an institution.

The level of skilled-care assistance is usually associated with acute injuries or illnesses. Occasionally, skilled care is necessary for individuals needing long-term care. Generally, long-term care is associated with non-skilled care (custodial) regardless of the environment where the care is received *(LTC Certificate Course Handbook)*.[28]

Likewise, according to Investopedia's definition, "custodial care" –at-home care is typically covered only under LTC insurance—not by Medicaid—even though home care is cheaper than a nursing facility. Medicare, on the other hand, only covers medically necessary skilled care and will cover

---

28 Corporation for Long-Term Care Certification (course handbook—October 2007, chapter 1. 26–27).

at-home custodial care only if it is provided in conjunction with skilled care (Investopedia.com).

Long-term care is almost exclusively custodial care, it's frequently described as supervisory or hands-on care assistance provided to individuals suffering from chronic illnesses or cognitive impairment. Individuals having physical impairments that limit or curtail their ability to perform simple, basic activities of daily living (ADLs) will create the need for custodial care. ADLs are personal-care involving bathing, dressing, continence, toileting, eating, and ambulation (transference or moving from one location to another).

According to the American Association of Retired Persons (AARP) in a 2005 report, the need for assistance with activities of daily living substantially increases with age. Note the following:

- An estimated eight percent (8%) of individuals between the ages of sixty-five and sixty-nine need assistance with basic activities of daily living.
- More than thirty-five percent (35%) of individuals at the age of eighty or greater will need daily assistance with the basic fundamentals of daily activities (*AOA and AARP-2005*).[29]

Custodial In-Home Care

On any given day, between twenty and fifty million Americans act as unpaid informal family caregivers, either in a part-time or a full-time capacity. The typical caregiver is a forty-six-year-old female caring for a parent(s), having a full-time career, and giving an average of eighteen hours of weekly care for one or more parents.

---

29 The Administration on Aging and AARP: A Profile of Older Americans. 2005, www.aoa.gov/PROF/Statistics/Profile /2005/Profiles2005.asp

Services rendered by typical custodial or unpaid family caregivers usually include broad homemaking duties and personal-care assistance as required by the individual. Homemaker assistance with instrumental activities of daily living (IADL) are provided to help an individual to remain in his or her home. IADL services frequently include light housework, laundry, meal preparation, kitchen maintenance, shopping for grocery items and personal necessities (Investopedia.com).[30]

Who Will Need LTC?

As Americans continue to age in record numbers, the need for comprehensive aging-in-place strategies contained within a long-term care plan has never been greater. The chart below, "The Third New Age," depicts an ever-increasing life expectancy for many Americans fueling the question still to be addressed, "Who will need long-term care? And have you formulated a long-term family care plan to stay in your own home?"

In 2010, forty million Americans were aged sixty-five years and older. By 2030, that number is estimated to reach seventy-two million people and according to a Robert Wood Johnson Foundation report in 2011, the nation spent more than $210 billion on long-term care services. The facts show that people today are living longer than seventy-five years ago when life expectancy was so limited there was not a concern for long-term care planning.

---

[30] www.Investopedia.com.

Table 1—The New Third Age
(---- Life Expectancy at Birth in The United States ----)

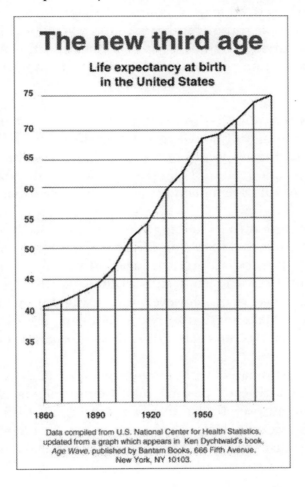

Today, according to scholar Ken Dychtwald, most Americans living to age sixty-five are expected to live another two decades. It's clear many Americans are living longer than ever before, but will you enjoy an active quality of life living two decades longer? What are the odds you'll need long-term care assistance? What are the odds you'll remain healthy and unscathed by a chronic or cognitive condition that will impair your quality of life?

As healthy individuals today live active lifestyles, it's difficult to imagine or predict a future day and time when people will no longer need hands-on assistance to perform basic living activities. People routinely take for granted activities like bathing or getting dressed. Thus, people often avoid the unpleasant thought and simply cease thinking about the subject and their future.

The facts remains that "seventy percent (70%) of individuals living to the age of sixty-five will require some type of care services at a future point in their life" (*LongTermCare.Gov*).[31] As married couples the odds increase exponentially that at least one spouse will have a need for long-term care services.

It can be argued that the bigger unknown is ascertaining the length of time in which one might need long-term care. It's virtually impossible to predict. One individual may need only a few months of care, while still another may need a couple of years of care services. However, increasingly individuals with dementia or Alzheimer's disease are requiring twenty-four-hour care for as long as ten years (*Transamerica Insurance Co*).[32]

The costs associated with long-term care services continue to increase with each passing year. Being diligent and saving for retirement over the course of a career can lead to a nice retirement lifestyle. However, having to pay for long-term care services for just a few years can threaten a financial nest egg that took decades to accumulate.

---

31 www.LongTermCare.Gov (The Basics. paragraph 1).
32 Transamerica Insurance Co. (www.TransamericaInsurance.com/associates_article.asp.id=66).

Key Determinants for Developing/Formulating an Aging-in-Place, Long-Term Care Plan—What Adults Need to Know

Why Is LTC Planning Critical?

Many Americans with increasing life expectancy are realizing, for the first time in their lives, a day of reckoning may come when they will no longer be able to care for themselves. In fact, at the turn of the twentieth century, the average life expectancy in the United States was a mere forty-six years of age *(Dychtwald)*.[33] Thus, for the vast majority of adults, long-term care planning was a phenomenon they would never encounter as death would occur long before frailty and age rendered them helpless and needing long-term care services.

For many individuals that have dealt with an extended long-term care episode involving a family member, they are all too well aware that long-term care issues do not bring families together. Rather, they tear families apart and cause great harm to decade long relationships between siblings, in-laws, or even new spouses. Where divorce has taken place, a whole new paradigm of issues can develop. For example, an adult child may voice objection at his or her future inheritance being spent for care involving a step-parent that has a serious illness or disability.

Long-term care planning can often alleviate the tremendous physical and emotional burdens associated with providing care while reducing the financial impact of rising care costs and family strife. Even with the accumulation of retirement assets over decades of working, most Americans are ill-equipped for the reality of long-term care costs and unexpected medical conditions that may occur.

---

33 Ken Dychtwald (www.agewave.com).

A 2013 "Cost of Care" survey conducted by John Hancock revealed the following:

- The average annual nursing home cost in the nation was to be in excess of $90,000 ($94,200).
- For those healthy enough to reside in assisted living facilities, the average annual cost exceeded $40,000 ($41,100).
- In-home health care services averaged just under $30,000 ($29,600) annually for six hours of daily care throughout a week (*National Clearinghouse for LTC Information*).[34]

Not having a plan for extended care can have devastating consequences for those you love. At a basic level, long-term care planning will protect your most important assets—your spouse and family.

LTC Health Consequences and the Trifecta of Unhealthy Outcomes

Although many Americans are living longer than ever before, the harsh reality is that we as a society have not made strides to improve our overall health outcomes. More and more Americans of all ages in this modern-day era are facing a health crisis. For many Americans, infectious diseases, acute illnesses, chronic diseases, and degenerative illnesses have made us a nation of less-healthier people.

---

[34] US Department HHS—National Clearinghouse for LTC Information. September 2008.

Looking inside, the numbers show the following:

- One in two adults had a chronic disease condition, and one of every four adults have multiple chronic health conditions *(Ward, Schiller, Goodman).*[35]
- With the prevalence of disability and chronic diseases increasing with age, seventy percent (70%) of people who reach age sixty-five will require long-term care services in some form during their later years. (JCHS—"Housing American's Older Adults: Meeting the Needs of an Aging Population").
- According to the same JCHS report, one in four older adults have a cognitive, hearing, mobility, or vision-impairment difficulty. By age eighty-five, more than two in three older adults will face at least one of these difficulties.

The challenge for many people today is having the knowledge, commitment, and wisdom to promote a healthy lifestyle as a top priority. Living a healthy lifestyle will foster greater independence helping to secure one's quality of life with age. Managing unhealthy behaviors plays a critical role in this process.

Living healthy is a lifestyle practice. Unfortunately, in this modern-day era, there are three key areas that will lead to unhealthy outcomes if not managed properly. Managing these challenges can significantly improve the quality of life for adults as they age and strive to remain independent. The three lifestyle challenges, which I refer to as the trifecta of unhealthy outcomes, are managing/preventing chronic disease conditions, maintaining cognitive health, and preventing unintentional injuries. These three lifestyle challenges will be further discussed in upcoming online workshops.

---

35 Ward, Schiller, Goodman. Multiple chronic conditions among US adults: 2012 update. *Preventing Chronic Disease.* 2014;11:130389.DOI.

Long-Term Care - Women's Issue

Why should women plan ahead? Two words are the answer: longevity and caregiving! Women live longer than men by an average of about five years. Moreover, married women tend to outlive their husbands, and women have higher rates of disability and chronic health problems.

Women are simply far more likely to need long-term care services. As shown in the facts and statistics below, women clearly need to have a comprehensive long-term care plan. Many are impoverished as a result of improper aging-in-place planning or financial debt left behind by a deceased husband.

Women are the principal caregivers. When their husbands need long-term care, wives are there providing the necessary services. Unfortunately, because many women are widowed, there is no one there to attend to their own long-term care needs if a family member is unavailable because of distance.

If you are a woman living alone (single, divorced, widowed), it is especially important that you embrace long-term care planning for your future. If you are a married woman whose husband is reluctant to spend the money for whatever reason, let a third party professional come in to talk about life-care and end-of-life planning needs. A long-term care insurance professional can show you how both plans can benefit you.

The issues for women come down to these key factors:

- Women live longer and, if married, will outlive their husbands.
- Women most likely will live alone, or women will be the principal caregivers for loved ones.
- Women who reach age sixty-five can expect to live an average of twenty more years, and those who reach age seventy-five can live an additional thirteen years.

- A third (33 percent) of long-term care insurance claims begin between ages seventy and seventy-nine; over half (55 percent) begin after age eighty.
- More than two-thirds of Americans ages eighty-five and older are women *(National Clearinghouse for LTC Information).*[36]
- Eight out of ten centenarians are women *(Dychtwald).*[37]
- Women spend twice as many years in a disabled state as men. At the end, they live 2.8 years longer if they live past sixty-five and 3.0 years more if they live past eighty.
- More than seventy percent (70%) of nursing home residents are women. The average age at admission is eighty.
- Three-fourths (75.7 percent) of residents in assisted living communities are women. Their average age at admission is eighty-five.
- Almost two-thirds of formal (paid) home care users and informal (unpaid) care recipients are women.
- Among people age seventy-five and older, women are sixty percent (60%) more likely than men to need help with one or more activities of daily living such as eating, bathing, dressing, or getting around their home *(National Clearinghouse for LTC Information).*[38]
- Almost seventy percent (70%) of women age seventy-five and older are widowed, divorced, or never married (compared to about thirty percent (30%) of men). This differential in marital status is very important.
- Women are more likely to live alone, having no one in their households to help with daily activities or provide support.

---

36 US Deparment HHS—National Clearinghouse for LTC Information. September 2008.

37 Ken Dychtwald (www.agewave.com).

38 US Department HHS—National Clearinghouse for LTC Information. September 2008.

- Nearly half (48%) of women age seventy-five and older are living alone, compared to less than one quarter (22%) of men.
- For women age seventy-five and older and living alone, the median household income is about $14,600 (2005). Married couples have a median household income of $35,000 (*AALTCI*).[39]

On a final note, elderly women are more likely than men to run out of resources later on in life. Divorced or separated women are the most vulnerable, because they have lower incomes and fewer resources.

The share of elderly women living in poverty is thirty-seven percent (37%) for divorced or separated, twenty-eight percent (28%) for widowed, twenty-two percent (22%) for never married, and ten percent (10%) for married. When women become caregivers, they are 2.5 times more likely to end up in poverty and 5 times more likely to depend on Social Security.

Why Purchase a Long-Term Care Policy?

More than once, an individual has posed what seems like a reasonable question, "Why should I purchase a long-term care policy that I may never use?" The question seems to have merit. Let's dig a little deeper to determine if it's the right question to ask.

People engaged in planning their future routinely protect their financial risk and personal assets through various insurance products. People purchase homeowner's insurance to protect their most prized possessions—their homes. Protecting such a sizable investment by insuring it against loss is not only prudent but good common sense.

---

[39] American Association for Long-Term Care Insurance (www.AALTCI.org).

Likewise when consumers purchase a new car with all the bells and whistles, they naturally insure it against loss. No one would think of making such an expensive purchase without insuring it against accidents or theft.

Guarding against the risk of financial ruin and loss is why people for generations have purchased life insurance. Protecting the life of the primary breadwinner to provide financial resources for the family in the event of a premature death seems elementary. Moreover, purchasing health insurance for self and family to eliminate risk and reduce financial hardship for a family has been common for years.

People have been protecting themselves and their families for good reasons over the years. All too often, tragedy strikes when it is least expected. It can be argued that prudent financial planning involves protecting assets like a home, automobile, one's personal health or life with various insurance products.

Now, the questions that one must ask: "What plan has been developed to protect your most important assets—your family and your personal independence? Likewise, is staying in the comfort of your own home important? And, who will care for you if you need help with some basic living activities?"

Retirement assets can be depleted virtually overnight to pay for extended facility or in-home care due to a loved one's medical or cognitive impairment. When the cost for care equates to tens of thousands of dollars a year, it is prudent to plan for the unexpected.

Where Do We Go from Here?

Without question, there are costs associated with long-term care—financial, emotional, and physical. Smart money management says that having a long-term care plan and funding that plan in either part or total with the purchase of a long-term care insurance product is prudent. The math is quite simple. If you live a long life, which demographic trends suggest is becoming the norm; you will eventually reach a time in your life when you will need assistance in managing the daily tasks of life.

Becoming frail and needing assistance does not have to be a daunting end-of-life scenario for consumers. A little planning and an honest evaluation of retirement assets and desired lifestyle can alleviate the costs with regard to long-term care.

Finally, there are several benefits of having a comprehensive aging-in-place plan with an emphasis on long-term care needs:

- An unexpected medical condition can occur anytime in life, and having a plan to help mitigate the family's financial, physical, and emotional caregiving duties and responsibilities is priceless.
- Long-term care policies will allow you extended time to stay in the comfort of your own home and remain in the community of your choice.
- There is peace of mind in knowing that health care agencies and other in-home service professionals are covered under long-term care policies and can be paid to help attend to your needs or those of an elderly parent.
- A long-term care policy can alleviate the stress, guilt, and frustration that come from being unable to care for an elderly parent due to work, time, and distance constraints.

CHAPTER 15

Module Component #6
Legal and Life-Care Planning

People Don't Plan to Fail, They Fail to Plan
—Miles Hurley
Elder care law attorney

What Is Elder Care and Elder Care Law?

The sixth core lifestyle component for aging gracefully to stay and live comfortably in your own home and community is turning to an elder care attorney for help and assistance. Whether it is your personal situation or that of a loved one—spouse, relative, or friend—you will need legal advice to navigate through a complex maze of eldercare rules and regulations.

The family needs to take care of their long-term care future by planning early rather than reacting to crisis. Most assuredly, there will be unexpected medical and financial issues that will rob you of your independence as you age. Therefore, pre-planning and having legal representation to guide you through this difficult maze will help you prepare a smart family plan to age-in-place.

What is elder care? And why do you need an elder care attorney? First, elder care, sometimes called elderly care or long-term care, refers to a wide array of services older people need as a result of age-related physical or mental impairment. (Investopedia.com/terms/e/elder-care). These services are provided for people who need help performing normal daily-living activity functions.

Elder care services provided by reputable professionals can include rehabilitative therapies, skilled nursing care, palliative care, and other social and senior-care services. These enhanced agency services can be provided in the home or outside the home.

In the home, unpaid family caregivers— usually family members, a spouse, a sibling, a relative, or a friend—are providing a brunt of personal-care services for the family and loved ones. A Pew Research Center report shows thirty-nine percent (39%) or one in three of US adults are caregivers. This is up from thirty percent (30%) as reported in 2010 *(Fox, Duggan and Purcell)*.[40],[41]

Why Do You Need an Elder Care Attorney?

Elder law attorneys specialize in a wide variety of areas. The goal is to help people weave through the legal maze to obtain the best available care for aging loved ones.

When it comes to aging matters, taking action for planning ahead is key. Elder law attorneys can assess and prepare legal documents, protect financial assets, discuss cost benefits for selling one's home, and calculate payment options for independent living and assisted living communities. Likewise, an elder law attorney can help provide the necessary information,

---

[40] "Part 1-Health Information Specialist" by Fox, Duggan, Purcell. (Pew Research Center: June 2013).

[41] "Family Caregivers are Wired for Health" by Fox, Duggan, Purcell. (Pew Research Center: June 2013).

resources, and other professional service referrals to help you in your decision-making process.

Planning ahead to have all legal obligations pertaining to personal health care, long-term care, and end-of-life matters is of great importance to an elder law attorney. Today, most elder law attorneys provide advice and guidance in a wide variety of areas including but not limited to:

- Advance directives for health care
- Elder abuse and fraud
- End-of-life planning
- Estate planning
- Guardianship and conservatorship
- Health care and mental health
- Nursing homes
- Medicaid and Medicare changes
- Planning for incapacity and long-term care
- Power of attorney
- Social Security
- Veteran aid and attendance benefits
- Wills, trusts, and probates

The legal aspects of planning and administration of healthcare, benefits, and personal assets are complex and difficult to navigate. Elder law attorneys can assist in developing a comprehensive elder care plan that integrates with an estate plan to help the family prepare for future elder care conflicts and financial issues.

Taking proactive legal planning action can mean the difference in being prepared for changes or being totally surprised. Therefore, planning ahead will help optimize the preservation of the family's lifetime savings and home. Through your knowledge and awareness. An elder care attorney can help identify the best course of action and decisions for you and your loved ones as you age.[42]

---

42 See more at http://www.hurleyeclaw.com/questions-and-answers/#sthash.okglIIS6.dpuf.

Life-Planning Process: Start Early and Plan Ahead

When it comes to aging and life-care planning, the number one challenge for everyone, regardless of age, is starting the process of planning early on in life. Planning ahead is of great importance for families who want to protect their futures when life circumstances change due to a chronic illness or disability.

An elder law attorney is one of several life-care professionals who can help plan a course of action to secure your and your loved one's independence. From estate planning to preparing legal documents for health care to finding caregiving support and services, an elder law attorney can help provide the information and resources to utilize in the decision-making process.

When it comes to planning ahead, there seems to be three principal planning processes for aging-in-place. They are: (1) life-care planning, (2) aging-in-place planning, and (3) estate planning. Let's look at these planning processes from a layman's viewpoint.

Life-Care Planning

Life-care planning is a process usually facilitated by an elder law attorney. Life-care planning is simply a customized legal document emphasizing long-term care concerns for aging-in-place. A life-care plan provides specific information about your and your spouse's health, your request for family-caregiving support, and financial resources that will help take care of yourself and your spouse to age gracefully in the comforts of your own home and community.

Life-care planning began as a field involving personal injury litigation. The intent at that time was to provide costs of care, equipment, supplies, and other services resulting from an injury. Life-care planning has evolved over the years and has moved beyond just injury litigation into a more comprehensive quality of life focus.

Today, life-care planning is a relationship with an elder care law practice that places special emphasis on concerns about long-term care for you and your spouse or elderly parent. A life-care plan can provide the roadmap to secure one's quality of life, including long-term care and financial goals and arrangements for where and how you want to be cared for in your later years.

A life-care plan can and will change over time as individual and family circumstances change. A viable plan attempts to look at your health, your family, your current needs, services, financial resources, and other resources that are available. The outcome sought is to maintain a comfortable quality of life as you age.

A life-care plan should encompass five planning goals:

1. Help provide assurances by first addressing, you and your spouse's health, safety, and well-being for maintaining a comfortable and independent quality of life (living) in later years.
2. Ensure that you or your loved one gets good care, whether that care is provided at home or outside the traditional home setting.
3. Help minimize family strife and contentions in making decisions relating to long-term care and special services when cognitive abilities become compromised or impaired.
4. Identify financial resources and services to pay for (1) in-home care or (2) long-term care in a senior living center or assisted living community.
5. Have end-of-life, prepaid burial arrangements and resources set aside for both you and your surviving spouse so that family members are not saddled with unnecessary funeral expenses.

Aging-in-Place Planning

Aging-in-place planning (AIPP) is a comprehensive, multifaceted, targeted approach that focuses on creating a quality-of-life action strategy for staying healthy and living independently with age. AIPP is a detailed process of collaborating and coordinating with family and loved ones a personal continuum of care addressing your caregiving requests and instructions, financial and legal assistance, home assessment/remodeling, long-term care, health services, healthy-eating practices, and more.

The goal of AIPP is to focus awareness on lifestyle challenges and the necessity to start early formulating smart family plans to age-in-place. The intent of the action strategy is to address and emphasize lifestyle behaviors that will afford everyone, regardless of age an opportunity to maintain good health outcomes to gracefully age-in-place.

Aging-in-place planning is much more than describing a process for the elderly to live and stay in the comforts of their own homes and communities. AIPP is an ongoing lifestyle practice focusing on healthy behaviors and activities to make health a top priority. The planning process starts early as teenagers and young adults moving forward in life by giving credence to health as the focus for achieving a better quality of life in later years.

Several Unique Aspects of the Aging-in-Place Planning Process (AIPP)

1. AIPP is an intervention that educates people of all ages about ways to live better, safely, and independently.
2. AIPP focuses on living healthy and promoting values, and decisions that make health a top priority.
3. AIPP educates people about effectively managing their chronic disease conditions (illnesses). Chronic disease

conditions affect one out of every two Americans and are a major cause for disease, premature death, and disability in the United States.
4. AIPP conducts home-area assessments for people who are considering downsizing or expanding living accommodations for extended family members (parent / grandparent / relative).
5. AIPP also highlights home-area improvements to make the home safer by reducing home-area hazards to prevent trips, slips, and fall injuries.
6. AIPP assesses and provides tools and tips to understand the complex family-caregiving dynamics and forces at work causing family disagreements.

These are just a few aspects of a comprehensive and multifaceted AIPP-targeted intervention that starts the process of formulating smart family plans to age-in-place. AIPP along with life-care planning and estate planning are the important processes that will afford you and your family an opportunity to start formulating smart family plans to live actively and healthy now in order to gracefully age-in-place later.

Estate Planning

Estate planning is the process of anticipating and arranging for the disposal of an estate. An estate plan attempts to ensure your assets are distributed according to your wishes. In addition, having an attorney who understands estate tax laws is critical for protecting wealth available to transfer to the next generations.

Estate planning attempts to eliminate uncertainties over the administration of a probate and maximize the value of the estate by reducing taxes and other expenses. The ultimate goal of an estate plan is to: 1) determine the specific goals and needs of the client, and 2) assess all available tax provisions to allow the client to claim a large share of what they've spent a lifetime building.

You should consult with a professional tax or legal advisor to formulate your estate plan. Let's begin with an overview of some basic estate planning questions you should ask before implementing any estate planning strategies:

Consider these three basic estate planning questions:

1. Who should inherit your assets?

If you are married, before you can decide who should inherit your assets, you must consider marital rights. States have different laws designed to protect surviving spouses. If you die without a will or living trust, state law will dictate how much passes to your spouse. Even with a will or living trust, if you provide less for your spouse than what the state law deems appropriate, the law will allow the survivor elect to receive the greater amount.

Once you have considered your spouse's needs, ask yourself these questions:

- Should your children share equally in your estate?
- Do you wish to include grandchildren or others as beneficiaries?
- Would you like to leave any assets to charity?

2. Which assets should they inherit?

You may want to consider special questions when transferring certain types of assets.

Consider these following examples:

- If you own a business, should the stock pass only to your children who are active in the business? Should you compensate the others with assets of comparable value?

- If you own rental properties, should all beneficiaries inherit them? Do they all have the ability to manage property? What are the cash needs of each beneficiary?
- Who gets the house, car, and important family heirlooms?

3. When and how should they inherit the assets?

To determine when and how your beneficiaries should inherit your assets, you need to focus on three factors:

- The potential age and maturity of the beneficiaries
- The financial needs of you and your spouse during your lifetimes
- The tax implications

Outright bequests? Offer simplicity, flexibility, and some tax advantages, but realize you have no control over what the recipient does with the assets once transferred. Trusts can be useful when the beneficiaries are young or immature, when your estate is large, and for tax planning reasons. They also can provide the professional asset-management capabilities an individual beneficiary lacks.

Financial Aid and Benefits for Seniors

Financial planning has changed dramatically over the years. Many people are outliving their funds or an unexpected medical disability, is eviscerating their retirement savings. Who will pay for the long-term care bills?

An excellent place to start planning is investing in a long-term care insurance product as outlined in chapter 14 of this book. In addition, maximizing retirement benefits offered by your employer and consulting with a financial advisor to create a personal savings and investment plan are options.

It's important to stress again that in long-term care planning, there is a tendency for the typical family to believe that an immediate family member will be the solution to future caregiving needs and assistance. Note, immediate family members and adult children are transient people (some living hundreds or thousands of miles from their parents)--and because of time, distance, and other restraints, they may be unable to care for you.

What are financial aid benefits for seniors to explore?

- **Wartime Veterans Aid and Attendance Benefits**[43]

    Most people think of veterans' benefits as being only for servicemen and servicewomen who were wounded or disabled while serving in the armed forces. In fact, the aid and attendance benefit is available to wartime veterans and their spouses who are now seniors and facing long-term care expenses such as home caregiving costs, assisted living facility fees, and nursing home expenses.

    There are now over twenty-five million US veterans eligible for VA benefits. Most believe they are only entitled to benefits if they were wounded or disabled while they were serving in the armed forces. Few vets realize that VA special pensions exist including the aid and attendance pension.

    Many vets are battling chronic conditions and medical illnesses, and they are struggling to pay for their care. VA special pensions are just one tool that an elder law attorney can look to when helping people plan for their long-term care needs.

---

[43] See more at http://www.hurleyeclaw.com/questions-and-answers/#sthash.okglIIS6.dpuf.

While you struggle to provide dignified, long-term care for a wartime veteran or surviving spouse, elder care professionals can help you understand what the options are and how to access underutilized benefits available to veterans.

- **VA Aid and Attendance Benefits**[44]

Aid and attendance is a special monthly pension available to wartime veterans and surviving spouses of wartime veterans. Aid and attendance is not a stand-alone benefit but is awarded on top of either the service benefit or the housebound benefit.

The veteran or surviving spouse must first be eligible for the service benefit. That requires the veteran serve at least ninety days of active military duty. At least one of those days had to be during wartime as defined by the Veterans Administration (*www.benefits.va.gov/*), and he or she had to receive a discharge other than dishonorable.

Most veterans, of course, receive honorable discharges. Additionally, there are many people who served in capacities that were not specifically in the army, navy, or air force who are included in VA benefits. Next, the veteran or surviving spouse must have a permanent and total disability or be over sixty-five.

Amazingly, the VA rates all veterans over the age of sixty-five, as permanently and totally disabled. For veterans under the age of sixty-five, permanent and total disability includes: being in a nursing home, being rated as disabled by the Social Security Administration, being unemployable and reasonably

---

44 See more at http://www.hurleyeclaw.com/questions-and-answers/#sthash.okglIIS6.dpuf.

certain to continue so throughout life, or suffering from a disability that makes it impossible for the average person to stay gainfully employed.

Once these initial hurdles have been cleared, the veteran or surviving spouse may be entitled to the aid and attendance pension. Please remember that aid and attendance is a level of pension and that there is no requirement of a service-connected disability.

- **The Process and VA Monthly Benefits**

In general, it takes six to nine months to start receiving VA benefits once the application has been submitted. The application can only be submitted once the client or the family has given all the information and documentation needed.

Once all requirements are met, the maximum monthly benefit is $2,019 for a married couple, $1,703 for a single veteran, or $1,094 for a surviving spouse. Children of a surviving wartime vet are not entitled to receive VA benefits.[45]

- **Medicaid Benefits**

Medicaid benefits work pretty much the same, though the process is faster. In order to apply for Medicaid, the client has to have been in a facility for thirty days. If the family has provided all the information and documentation needed, then an application can be submitted.

The state/county in which the application has been submitted has forty-five business days to respond, and

---

45 See more at http://www.hurleyeclaw.com/questions-and-answers/#sthash.okglIIS6.dpuf.

the application is usually approved within several months. Once the Medicaid application has been approved, it will pay for the nursing home up to three months prior to the approval.

Please consult your elder law attorney to obtain more information and other benefits available to veterans.

Medicare and Medicaid Overview

Medicaid is a joint federal and state program that helps with medical costs of people with limited income and resources (HealthCare.gov). Medicaid covers medical care such as doctor visits and hospital costs, long-term care services in nursing homes, and long-term care services provided at home (visiting nurses and assistance with personal care). Medicaid eligibility is limited by personal income and is generally limited to the following:

- People aged sixty-five years and older
- Children under nineteen
- Pregnant women
- People living with a disability
- Parent or adult caring for a child
- Adult without dependent children (in certain states)
- Eligible immigrant

Medicaid may also cover the following services not normally covered by Medicare:

- Nursing home services for all eligible people aged twenty-one years and older.
- Home and community-based services for people who would need to be in a nursing home.
- Personal-care services, case management, and help with laundry and cleaning (this is usually referred to as

custodial-care services) for eligible clients remaining in their home.

Note: Most Medicaid and public health long-term care programs cover custodial care as long as they are provided in a nursing care facility. Typically, custodial care in the home is covered under LTC insurance (long-term care insurance policy).

- Medicaid will not pay for rent, mortgage, utilities, or food.

Each state has different rules about eligibility requirements and applying for Medicaid. Check to see whether your state Medicaid program offers alternatives to nursing home care services.

According to the Centers for Medicare and Medicaid Services (US government, Medicare handbook—"Medicare and You" 2015), Medicare is a government-run health insurance for people aged sixty-five years and older, people under sixty-five with certain disabilities, and people of any age with end-stage renal disease (ESRD), a permanent kidney failure requiring dialysis or a kidney transplant.

Generally, Medicare is divided into two parts with the first part of coverage (part A) encompassing the following:

- In-patient hospitalization
- Home health and hospice care
- Skilled nursing facility
- Some preventive services

The second part of coverage (part B) encompasses almost all necessary medical services such as the following:

- Doctor's services
- Laboratory and x-ray services

- Outpatient care
- Home health care
- Durable medical equipment (wheelchairs, shower grab bars, etc.)
- Some preventive services

Also, part of Medicare is the Medicare part D, Medicare prescription drug coverage. This part D section helps cover the cost of prescription drugs by Medicare-approved private insurance companies. The intent of this service is to lower prescription drug costs and protect against higher drug costs in the future.

Medicare and Long-Term Care

> *At least 70% of people over 65 will need long-term care services and support at some point in their life.*[46]
> —US DHHS (www.LongTermCare.gov)

As discussed in chapter 14, long-term care services include medical and nonmedical care provided to people who are unable to perform basic activities of daily living due to a chronic health illness or disability. Basic activities of daily living include dressing, bathing, eating, ambulation, and toiletry.

Long-term care support and services can be provided at home, in the community, in assisted living facilities, or in nursing homes. However, Medicare and most health insurance plans do not pay for long-term care, which is sometimes referred to as custodial care. Therefore, it's important to start planning for long-term care needs early in life to ensure that you and your loved ones can maintain personal dignity and independence as you age-in-place.

---

46 US DHHS (www.LongTermCare.gov)

Long-term care can be provided and paid for in a variety of ways. Below are some options from the U.S. Government, Medicare Handbook – *Medicare & You* 2015.[47] (8)

> *Long-term care insurance*—This type of private insurance can help pay for many types of long-term care, including both skilled and non-skilled (custodial) care. Long-term care insurance policies can vary widely. Some policies may cover only nursing home care. Others may include coverage for a range of services, like adult day care, assisted living, medical equipment, and informal home care. Note: A long-term care insurance policy does not replace your Medicare coverage.
>
> *Personal resources*—Many people choose to use their own resources to pay for long-term care. Keep in mind that long-term care can be very expensive. It is important to know the financial risks before you decide to try to save enough money on your own. You should discuss your specific situation with your family members and a financial professional.
>
> *Other private options*—Some insurance companies allow you to use your life insurance policy to pay for long-term care. Ask your insurance agent how this works. Also, you may choose to pay for long-term care through a trust or annuity. The best option for you depends on your age, health status, risk of needing long-term care, and personal financial situation. Visit LongTermCare.gov for more information about your options.
>
> *Medicaid*—Medicaid is a joint federal and state program that helps pay for certain health services for people with limited income and resources. If

---

47 US government, Medicare handbook—"Medicare and You" 2015.

you qualify, you may be able to get help to pay for nursing home care or other health care. Medicaid services may also help you stay in your home. For more information, contact your state.

Veterans' benefits—The Department of Veterans Affairs (VA) may provide long-term care for service-related disabilities or for certain eligible veterans. The VA also has a housebound aid and attendance allowance program that provides cash grants to eligible disabled veterans and surviving spouses. For more information, visit va.gov, or call the VA at 1-800-827-1000. TTY users should call 1-800-829-4833.

Important Elder Care Legal Documents

Families who are caring for an elderly parent or contemplating caregiving service should have an attorney prepare several legal documents long before the parent starts having trouble handling certain aspects of his or her life. Life circumstances can quickly change someone's ability to care for himself or herself, especially if a cognitive impairment (disability) is suspected.

Therefore, it's important to note that aging parents may not want to relinquish authority right away. However, over time, a child whom the parents believe is the most trusting and responsible one can usually persuade the reluctant parent that having a proxy is in their best interest.

A durable power of attorney (POA) enables the elderly parent (called the principal in the power of attorney document) to appoint an agent, such as a trusted adult child, relative, or friend, to handle specific health, legal, and financial responsibilities.

There are two types of power of attorney (POA) documents:

- POA for health-care gives a designated person the authority to make health-care decisions on behalf of the parent/person.
- POA for finances gives a designated person the authority to make legal/financial decisions on behalf of the parent/person.

Next, an advance health care directive is technically a state's advance directive for health care. This document could include designating someone to be a health care agent or to be a health care power of attorney.

In summary, to designate someone to handle your money, you would complete a durable power of attorney for financial matters. Durable means that the power of attorney remains effective even if a person becomes incapacitated. In other words, an advance directive is for health-care matters, whereas a power of attorney is for financial and property matters.

In addition, in most states many people have or previously had a living will and a durable power of attorney for health-care. The living will is a legal document allowing an individual to choose whether or not he or she wants to die naturally without death being artificially prolonged by various medical procedures. The living will is an authorization to your medical professionals to withhold or withdraw certain medical procedures such as a ventilator, respirator, feeding tube, hydration solution, and pain medication.

The durable power of attorney for health care is a legal document appointing and naming another person to make health-related decisions on one's behalf, and it gives this person called the agent some idea of what you may or may not want regarding potential medical procedures that may need to be administered in the future.

In the State of Georgia, the advance directive for health care now provides the designated proxy the rights to control all aspects of his or her medical care including the right to insist on medical treatment and request for it to be withdrawn, or to refuse treatment. The new legal document allows individuals to appoint an agent to make a medical-treatment decision if direct communication is not possible, and it authorizes an individual's medical professionals to withhold or withdraw certain treatments or procedures.

Special Summary Note

Please consult your elder law attorney or other professionals to obtain more information about legal and life-care planning matters. I have compiled just a brief summary of some issues for you to consider; however, this does not represent all elder care matters.

Also, make sure you and your parents have a will. *Will, Trust, and Probate* issues were not discussed here. These important matters should be discussed with an elder law attorney. Keep all legal documents in a secure place, and make sure a responsible family member is made aware of their location.

CHAPTER 16

Module Component #7
Family Dynamics of Caregiving

The Family-Caregiving Culture

When it comes to caring for elderly loved ones, every modern-day family has its own caregiving dynamics that cause strife and contention among family members. At the center of this family institution is the forever-changing structural dynamics of the modern-day family as we age. The traditional nuclear family as it first appears (husband, wife, and children living in a common household) is now becoming more of an extended-family household. Extended-family households now encompass three or more generations sharing living arrangements.

Today's modern-day families have to contend with a whole host of obstacles including geographic isolation, divorce, medical disabilities, addictions, elder caregiving, home safety, and employment opportunities. These obstacles may generate family disagreements as to who will be caring for you when your time comes. In an effort to help identify the various family dynamics of the in-home caregiving family culture, it is best to take time to better understand the family actions and forces at work.

Family-caregiving dynamics are the interactions and relationships that exist within a family. The dynamics of family functions and how families relate to one another over family-caregiving matters cannot be oversimplified. The family dynamics manifest in many ways when it comes to families caring for older adults and relatives.

This chapter lesson, "Family Dynamics of Caregiving," carefully attempts to highlight the modern-day family-caregiving culture and forces at work. The breakthrough sought is to understand the forces at work in order to minimize potential family-caregiving contentions. The outcome is to simply understand both the spiritual gift and family nuisances of an unpaid family caregiver.

Caring for an aging family member works best when everyone acts as a team; however, this is seldom the case. Conflicts will arise that are unexpected or may seem trivial. Be prepared for the contentions that will arise. Family contentions may manifest over such things as: division of labor, financial matters, loved one's health condition(s), and long distance caregiving[48].

Understanding Family Forces at Work

Let's assess your understanding of the family-caregiving forces at work. Every family has its own caregiving dynamics to contend with and minimizing potential conflicts requires a prescription of wisdom, temperance, love, and understanding.

The exercise below is intended to help you self-assess the structural dynamics of your family-caregiving interactions, relationships, actions, and habits. The sole intent of this exercise is to assess what you perceive as family forces causing contention, strife, and tribulations.

---

48   www.nia.nih.gov
     ("Long Distance Caregiving—A Family Affair")

Read the questions below and place the appropriate check mark, answering yes or no to the question. When you have finished this exercise, carefully review your answers. If there are more yes answers than no answers, then you have truly joined the ranks of the unpaid family caregiver. Here your frustrations take on an emotional cycle of grief: reckoning, guilt, denial, and anger.

The point of this exercise is for you to look at yourself and personally assess your family-caregiving dynamics and forces at work. This is not all on you to bear, for all family members contribute to the forces at work. It is up to you to understand these forces so you can focus on your personal behaviors and interactions that will allow you to provide the best personal care for aging loved ones.

The Family-Caregiving Exercise
Family Discourse at Work—Fostering Grief, Guilt, and Frustration

1. In the past twelve months, have you provided unpaid care to an adult relative or friend (eighteen years or older) to help them take care of themselves? (Yes or no)
2. Are there family meetings to discuss sibling roles, duties, finances, and responsibilities in planning the care of a parent(s)? (Yes or no)
3. Do you perceive that the *burden of care* for an aging parent (older adult) isn't distributed equally (usually one of the adult siblings, by default, takes on most of the caregiving duties and responsibilities)? (Yes or no)
4. Are there family discords and disagreements over finances involving medical matters and interventions needed (i.e., in arranging for outside services, who will pay for them and other practical issues)? (Yes or no)
5. Are there family discourse and contention over who will expand their household living accommodations to care for an aging parent? (Yes or no)

6. Are there disagreements and contention over parent condition(s) and capabilities and about what's wrong and what should be done about it (example: no longer capable of driving to maintain independence)? (Yes or no)
7. Are there sibling rivalries and favoritism dating back to childhood that you perceive as an issue? (Yes or no)
8. Are you prideful in not asking for help or needing and wanting help? (Yes or no)
9. Do you believe certain family members are only interested in the inheritance and how quickly they can get it? (Yes or no)
10. Do you believe your time is worth nothing when it gets to be too much and no one seems to notice or volunteers to take your place? (Yes or no)
11. Do you spend a significant amount of time each month planning and traveling to attend to elder care matters? (Yes or no)
12. Are there a sibling(s) or relative living with a parent or nearby in town that you believe is deceiving and depleting parent resources? Are you finding family heirlooms and mementos suddenly missing? (Yes or no)
13. Are you emotionally frustrated by wasting valuable time arranging for outside services and later having a parent make one-phone call to cancel the agreed-upon service? (Yes or no)
14. Are you the one making the end-of-life emergency decisions when there is not a living will or other advance directive? (Yes or no)

In summary, according to the Pew Research Center, some thirty-nine percent (39%) of US adults are caregivers, up from thirty percent (30%) in 2010 and about one-third of people in a home show survey reported they are contemplating caring for an older parent or relative (Atlanta Home Show Expo 2008—"Safe Home for Life" participant survey).

Keep in mind the unpaid family caregiver need not live with you. They are parents, siblings, relatives, or friends who help with personal needs or household chores. They may also manage finances, arrange for outside professional and social services, and make regular home visits to see how loved ones are doing.

For unpaid family caregivers, the emotional cycle of guilt and frustration is inevitable and real. Trying to maintain a healthy balance to care for others in the midst of family strife and contention requires love, patience, and understanding as prescribed earlier.

Taking a closer look at these forces, interactions, and relationships, let's see if there are some answers as to why individual family members do what they do. Reading the "Strange Family Story" will help you better understand family caregivers and the negative forces at work within families.

The Strange Family Story: Whipped for Caring

My aunt and uncle were not blessed with biological children, but they had several nieces and nephews who loved and adored them. I was the only niece that volunteered to be their caretaker during their senior years. Other nieces and nephews made themselves available upon request. Uncle Lew, as we called him, eighty-three, was like a father to me. It was a little awkward when our roles reversed. I became more like the parent, and he became the child.

I remember telling him I was not ready for him to die; he replied and told me, "Okay, I'll stay a little longer." Through all the visits with the doctors and hospital admittances from 2000 to 2003, he stayed strong and did everything he could to sustain his life. In the end, dialysis was too strong for his heart. He died after only a few dialysis treatments.

In the summer of 1998, Aunt Sadie was diagnosed with breast cancer. She initially did not want to cooperate with the doctors and did not inform the family of the diagnosis. I learned about the diagnosis in the fall of that year, and I somehow, convinced her to allow me to take her for a second opinion. The second opinion confirmed the diagnosis of her primary physician—breast cancer. She was scheduled for surgery within a week of the second opinion. She had a lumpectomy, followed by chemotherapy and radiation.

In 2002, she was diagnosed with gallbladder disease. Again, she did not want to cooperate with her doctor. I received a call from the family while at work. I immediately left my office and traveled three hours to Aunt Sadie and Uncle Lew's home. I called her as I was driving and stressed the importance of cooperating with the doctor. When I arrived at the house, the three of us (Aunt Sadie, Uncle Lew, and I) had a conversation about the seriousness of gallbladder disease. After the conversation, I took her to the doctor. She was immediately admitted to the hospital with surgery scheduled the following day.

She bounced back and lived a healthy and independent life until after Uncle Lew's death. A few years after his death in 2007, she was diagnosed with a rare disease—tumor on the pancreas. I took her to a specialist for a second opinion. Without surgery to remove the tumor, she would have died.

On the morning of her surgery, as we were leaving the house for the hospital, she told me she was not ready to die. We prayed and asked God to take care of her.

After returning home from the rehabilitation facility, she lived with me in Georgia during her recovery. At that time, she was about eighty-three years old. For as long as I knew her, she would have periods of great joy followed by depression. Since she was living with me, I decided to take her to a therapist.

She attended group therapy for twelve weeks and reported enjoying the conversations. Because I worked, I suggested she move to a nearby active senior community center so that she could regularly interact with other seniors and have three meals daily. She said no and decided to move back to her house in Alabama.

I was okay with her decision, because I knew my mother and her sister lived in the same community and they could be company for one another. I also arranged for another niece to visit Monday through Friday to prepare meals, help her with daily hygiene, and do light housekeeping. Living in another state, I was not able to visit daily but called regularly and visited about twice a month.

In January 2009, my mother's health started to decline. She had a brief hospital stay in December 2008. I started going home every other weekend and later every weekend to care for my mother and Aunt Sadie. Sadly, my mother died just before Easter. Another sister of Aunt Sadie moved in to help with her care; she stayed until late summer.

When Aunt Sadie's sister returned to her own home after the summer, I hired a caretaker, Clara, to visit Monday through Friday to prepare meals, help her with daily hygiene, and do light housekeeping. Aunt Sadie was initially reluctant to have someone help her, but after a couple of weeks, she looked forward to seeing Clara (Clara was the daughter of Aunt Sadie's good friend).

Not long after the death of my mother, Elvira, my seventeen-year-old niece who lived with my mother started visiting Aunt Sadie. It was not uncommon for my niece to visit Aunt Sadie once or twice a week.

I wasn't concerned about the increase in the visits; I concluded they were comforting each other after the loss of our loved one. I also knew that I was working to help Elvira get into college. I didn't know, however, that Elvira's visits were for financial reasons. This became apparent as I received daily calls from her asking for money. She always needed something—diapers and milk for her baby, gas, and more.

By the next year, Elvira was frequently getting in trouble for writing bad checks. I found myself doing what I later learned my mother did—paying for the bad checks. When I started to confront Elvira about the likelihood she was on drugs, I received pushback from several family members (people who had known me all my life).

I soon learned that Elvira was defaming my name and reputation to family and community members. She was quite convincing—sweet baby talk, always including a flood of tears with her stories.

She convinced Aunt Sadie that she was the only one who cared about her. Aunt Sadie believed her and immediately started spending her fixed income on Elvira. Elvira, in 2010, moved in with Aunt Sadie, ran the caretaker away, and managed to turn Aunt Sadie against me (first) and later her siblings and other family members.

At this point, we contacted Adult Protective Services (APS). For the next three years, APS made several visits to the home, but Aunt Sadie always denied there were problems. The neighbors, however, frequently described trouble in the house such as Elvira yelling at Aunt Sadie and running her away from her own home.

Aunt Sadie stopped all annual medical visits and living conditions became deplorable—all in the name of love. She decided it was her responsibility to pick up where my mother left off—take care of Elvira and her baby. She lost weight due to a poor diet, had scales on her skin from poor hygiene and lost most of her hair because she didn't have anyone to wash and take care of her. Everyone including family, friends, and community members felt helpless. APS and the police couldn't help. Aunt Sadie was very protective of Elvira.

Aunt Sadie became ill in 2013 and was taken to the emergency room. After a battery of tests, she was diagnosed with bladder cancer. The family again attempted to get her out of the house and away from Elvira, but Elvira was busy in the background telling Aunt Sadie that she was the only one who loved her and could take care of her.

When Aunt Sadie returned home from the hospital, the medical staff arranged for hospice care. With constant visits to the home by hospice and also APS, the family was able to reenter her life. We managed to get her out of the house and in an extended care facility. She died within three weeks of leaving the house at the age of eighty-eight. Her death certificate stated decubitus ulcers as the primary cause of death and malnutrition as secondary.

Unlike Uncle Lew who died with dignity, Aunt Sadie died at the hands of a selfish manipulator. I know that Aunt Sadie was aware of Elvira's drug addiction, but she believed she needed to protect Elvira's child. To do so meant she had to turn against the family. In the end, I think she came to realize she had taken on more than she could handle.

Behaviors Exhibited by Older Adults and Family Members

1. The Spirit of Independent Stubbornness

Strife and contention for many family members caring for older loved ones will definitely surface when stubbornness is at the root of behavior and family dysfunction.

First, a stubborn person is someone seen by others who refuses' to change his or her mind — despite being presented with what others consider are good reasons or facts to do so. Stubbornness, for many older adults, is a manifestation of a behavior that is often triggered by but not limited to these circumstances:

- Being treated as a child
- Feeling frustrated
- Not feeling well
- Reacting to a medication or food
- Not understanding what they were asked to do
- Not understanding what they thought, saw, or heard
- Being hurried
- Being cared for by someone who is often in a rush
- Needing to think about several things at once

Second, the spirit of independent stubbornness is an attitude, feeling, or mood that inspires a dual emotion—directing someone toward something or away from something. Two principle drivers (spirits) usually characterize this behavior: (1) a spirit rooted and grounded in selfishness and (2) a spirit rooted and grounded in love.

Selfishness can be both good and bad. A person, for example, who does not wish to smoke exercises a spirit of independent stubbornness. A sibling, likewise, who is an absentee family member from caregiving duties and responsibilities, also exercises the same spirit of independent stubbornness. The principal behaviors addressed in these two examples are one operating in a spirit of love for living healthy and the other operating in a spirit of selfishness (it's all about me).

1. The Alpha Sibling

Sibling strife and contention are the conflicts between brothers and sisters who want to exercise control or dominance when dealing with family matters. Keep in mind that this contention is not relegated to the oldest child or only child in the family. This strife and contention are usually a manifestation of a specific temperament to become the alpha leader—family advisor, leader, and executive.

Identifying individual sibling temperaments among family members is key for minimizing the dysfunctions that exist within families. All family members have a particular way of doing things. Therefore, it's up to siblings, in the absence of a rational parent and aging-in-place plan, to make caregiving decisions.

Identifying character traits is important, for not all siblings have the temperament to be a family caregiver. For example, the child who has the nature for being direct and to the point may not be the best caregiver for a parent.

The child who has the nurturing temperament—exercising moderation, self-control, forgiveness, mercy, and understanding—may be the best person for expanding his or her living accommodation to take in a parent. Likewise, the child who has a temperament of an organizer—structured, conscientious, cool, calm, and collected—has good caregiving character traits.

Family caregiving is a team approach. It calls upon and involves everyone within the family and sometimes solicits relatives and friends to participate. Remember not everyone, especially family members, will want to become part of a caregiving team. Some individuals have their own hidden agendas. The best advice: do not fret, just move on.

2. The Family Artist/Manipulator (A&M)

Every family has an individual or relative who is an expert in trickery and deceit—the family artist/manipulator. This is a person who skillfully engages in the psychological manipulation of others, usually the elderly. The A&M is a master manipulator of people, painting his or her picture of what they want you to see and hear.

The artist/manipulator uses a broad spectrum of social and emotional manipulations (actions) like underhandedness, deception, abuse, and exploitative tactics to perpetuate his or her own personal interest. They are true artists, often painting themselves as the victim to the most vulnerable, the elderly, and other outsiders.

The manipulator, as illustrated in the "Strange Story," gets what he or she wants through emotional manipulations. Guilt and sympathy are potent emotional instruments used by individuals to turn situations around in their favor. They are the master practitioners rationalizing, justifying, and explaining things their way.

The A&M, through subtle but covert aggressive actions, manipulates victims by trying to isolate them from other family members. They tend to move in and isolate their subjects by becoming the elderly's gatekeeper and caregiver often with a monetary purpose to fulfill.

Knowing the psychological vulnerabilities of the elderly, the A&M determines what tactics are likely to be most effective. They possess a sophisticated level of ruthlessness and have no qualms about mistreating people or causing harm to their victim if necessary (adult maltreatment).

3. The Enabler

The challenge for many family members and professional caregivers is walking that tightrope of being helpful and acting as enablers. Most family conflicts and contention center on someone's behavior as enabler—kindness exhibited in helping loved ones too much.

> *Ninety-six percent, 96%, of the general population, and persons in helping professions exhibit some forms of co-dependent behavior.*
> —Sharon Wegscheider-Cruse

We all have on occasion, observed a family member crossing that invisible line between being truly helpful and supportive and acting as enablers or being codependent with a loved one. Enabling is a source of contention when the motherly involvement, by nature, crosses the line and becomes counterproductive caring.

Family members, by nature, usually engage in some sort of co-dependence or enabling actions. This is seen when we routinely and unconsciously step in for an older adult to help them carry through on a basic activity for daily-living (ADL) function. Taking a closer look at this benevolent behavior is to define an enabler as the following:

> Enabling is a pattern of nurturing interactions that are intended to help shield someone from adverse outcomes or from consequences of his or her poor choices.

I find in my observations of family members and professional caregivers, interactions with older adults can often hinder loved ones from exercising independence. This occurs when we inadvertently step in to provide help and assistance instead of engaging our loved ones in self-actions and encouragement. This is a way of exercising their cognitive abilities. Being helpful to engage, interact, and influence outcomes is an important elder care brain-health activity for family caregivers to constantly stimulate.

Finally, are you helping (engaging loved ones) or hindering (being an enabler)? It's hard to see a loved one struggle to perform simple tasks when we could simply step in to assist them in the tasks. The constant and consistent need for hindering can cross the line for certain family members observing and may be a source of some contention.

Take this simple quiz to help you assess if you have enabler tendencies. Review the questions, and answer any item that pertains to you or that you have observed. Keep in mind that we all exhibit enabler tendencies. The goal is to engage loved ones in stimulation to maintain cognitive brain functions.

Enabling Quiz

1. When eating at a restaurant do you suggest or recite menu courses/meals instead of letting your loved ones decide?
2. Are you always moving (on-the-go) for your convenience or comfort in dealing with parents?
3. Do you often step in to provide activity for daily-living (ADL) assistance instead of asking permission to help?

4. Are you direct and impatient?
5. Are you quick to cut into/off a conversation because you already know what he/she is trying to say (not allowing loved ones to formulate a question or answer)?
6. Do you not operate with self-control or temperance?
7. Do you often oversee, run, and control others or just participate in a direct/aggressive way to save time?
8. Some parents retell stories over and over again. Do you let them tell the story or step in to abruptly or politely cut them off?

If you have answered yes to three or more of these questions, it is likely that you have crossed the line from being supportive to being an enabler or codependent.

5. The Denier

The reaction for some individuals in the family is to deny the reality that an elderly loved one has become ill and may need care-giving assistance. This is a normal defensive reaction of a grieving process. It's up to you to understand and neither judge nor take offense to their inward or outward emotions. It will take time for some family members to fully process the reality of a disability or cognitive impairment and admit to it. Deniers usually have to see things for themselves, personally spending time and seeing things firsthand.

Keep in mind that people respond differently when bad news hits them about their parents. The feeling of parents' invincibility and immortality has now been emotionally threatened and shattered. Many individuals coping with this hold steadfastly to blocking out the news and facts. Their approach is to think positive about the situation by adhering to an old saying: "As long as there is life ––there is hope. As long as there is hope –– there is life."

Understand that the emotional reaction may be a spiritual intervention. They may not want or give credence to the negative reality of the situation. They speak and often act positively to the expected outcome measure they expect through the spiritual grace that is already given to us. "By his stripes we are healed" (Isaiah 53:7, KJV). Denial helps people deal with grief in their own way. It's nature's way of letting us cope with emotions to simply get through each day.

6. The Helper—Responsible One

The adult child who assumes the role of the unpaid family caregiver for an elderly parent is most often described as the responsible one. Although each family unit and culture is unique, there are many family dynamics at play that can cause strife and contention between adult siblings caring for loved ones.

The responsible one, who is acting out of love and kindness, is most often working overtime attending to an aging parent, grandparent, or relative usually with a medical condition(s). The responsible one is usually the homemaker aide providing the aging parent(s) with emotional support, stability, and medical assistance. They give advice and guidance, handle financial matters, and provide the parent's transportation service to appointments and assist with groceries and other errands.

The common underlying causes of family friction among adult children are often over money, control, and unequal distribution of duties. In some cases, sibling distance and work responsibilities can become issues as well as siblings who are absent in the caregiving process. You have to engage them to help.

Discord among siblings is real and can have devastating effects on family interactions, on relations, and upon self (unneeded and unwarranted personal stress and strain).

Family conflict will also arise over the handling of a parent chronic disease condition/illness. Example, dealing with a parent with Alzheimer disease can bring out many strong emotions[49].

The temperament usually exhibited by the responsible one is that of a person who is organized, cool, and calm. They seek peace, harmony, and cooperation for the family to work together. They are the family members who are most dependable and reliable. This is not to say other siblings are not.

A MetLife 2011 report shows nearly ten million adult children over the age of fifty care for their aging parents. The average age of an unpaid family caregiver is forty-eight. Two-thirds, 66 percent, of unpaid family caregivers are women, married, mothers, and still working, as reported by the National Alliance of Caregiving and AARP 2009.

Family-Caregiving Solutions to Minimize Strife and Conflicts (Eight-Point Solution)

First and foremost, in an effort to bring awareness to young adults, baby boomers, family caregivers, and those contemplating caring for loved ones, it is best to become aware of the reckoning. Someday in the not-so-distant future, a question will be asked, "While caring for others, who will care for you?"

Developing an aging-in-place family-caregiving plan that focuses on and addresses the seven core family-caregiving principles for living healthy is the first step. The goal for all people of all ages is to make health a top priority. The outcome measures sought are to maintain independence to stay in your own home as you age.

Second, know that family conflicts will arise. There will be an array of interactions that will strain family relationships, pitting brothers against sisters or having parents show favoritism

---
49 www.alz.org ("Resolving Family Conflict"

towards one child. Note, some subtle contentions may also surface between an only child and family relatives or a divorced spouse.

Handling these situations with a heavy dose of temperance is crucial to surviving these family conflicts. Becoming that cool, calm, and organized person is key for mitigating family conflicts that will surely test your resolve. Therefore, let's give attention to some helpful family interactions as the unpaid family caregiver. These solutions may help minimize some strife and contention among family members:

The following solutions listed below are tips to minimize family strife and contentions. These tips are compiled from a compilation of sources including but not limited to: 1) The 50-50 Rule: *Solving Family Conflicts,* 2) Alzheimer Society, *When Families Do Not* Agree: *Strategies...in a supportive manner,* and 3) The Caregiver's Survival Handbook: *Caring for Your Aging Parent...Losing Yourself* (Abramson and Dunkin). Also see Dr. Alexis *expert advise – Avoiding Caregiver Conflict*[50]

> (1) www.alzheimer.ca/ottawa, Alzheimer Society of Ottawa and Renfrew County
> (2) www.solvingfamilyconflict.com- The 50/50 Rule: Solving Family Conflict
> (3) Abramson, A and Dunkin, MA, The Caregiver's Survival Handbook: *Caring for Your Aging Parents Without Losing Yourself,* February 2011.

Solutions for Minimizing Family Contentions

1. Begin a sensitive aging-in-place discussion with a parent(s): Do not wait until a sudden onset of a disability will exacerbate family strife and contention. Develop an aging-in-place family-caregiving plan, and seek buy-in

---

50 Abramson, A. and Dunkin, M. A.—*The Caregivers Survival Handbook* (2011)

from other family members. Also, don't lose sight of your parent's stubbornness may hinder the planning process.

2. Hold frequent family meetings: Start formulating an aging-in-place family-caregiving plan. The plan should address the seven core fundamental components for aging-in-place. The components have been outlined in this book—chapters 7–15. Note, aging-in-place principles are established for all people to implement. Someday, you will need a caregiver. So plan your work and work your plan.
3. Engage all family members, but know not all will be helpful: Starting early on engaging family members to take part in the planning process will cut down on some of the family contention. Parcel out responsibilities to various family members by critical core area components. Assign specific core area components to investigate by assessing and assigning duties to each family member.
4. Hold your criticism and avoid assumptions: Family meetings and personal discussions with family members will be necessary when sensitive issues are brought to the table. "Be positive and stay positive," is the motto to embrace. Keep in mind that some issues will depend on timing. Sometimes, it may be necessary to temporarily hold back issues from the group. Acknowledge the issues. Do not avoid the issues, but table discussion until a later date. Some family members may not be at an emotional state, place, and time to handle the gravity of the situation.
5. Show disgruntled siblings/relatives the inner circle: Certain siblings who are interested in promoting their own selves are looking for a payday. Getting their inheritance is more important to some siblings than doing the right thing—helping in the care of a parent. Siblings who seem absent or aloof from family matters are only interested in promoting their own agendas.

Usually, some form of addiction is at the root of the problem or a contentious brother/sister-in-law.

Implementing the old cliché, "Keep your friends close and your enemies closer" is your strategy to keep tabs on them. Keeping them in your inner circle to monitor their family comings and goings is key. As a reminder, these individuals are manipulators constantly turning family matters and situations to their personal interests, looking out for the family weak link, sibling, or relative to wield their web of deceit. Make friends with family malcontents, watch them and look out for flaws and weaknesses of individuals for them to exploit.

6. Prepare an inventory of heirlooms for memories: Family heirlooms, pictures, inheritances, and mementos all raise powerful emotional and financial attachments for family. Start now discussing with parents the whereabouts of important legal papers, insurance, and other documents.

   You and a family member together need to take an inventory of important heirlooms, pictures, and mementos that may or may not be specified in a will. Make the inventory list known to immediate siblings. It's important to take account of these items early, for over time, they will end up missing or taken by a sibling, sisters/brothers/in-laws, or a distant family relative.

7. Establish a circle support system: The circle support system starts with family. Start to identify and research with family members types of caregiving services, organizations, and resources that can help you care for loved ones. Often you will have to look beyond siblings

for help. Church members, faith ministries, relatives, veterans, and retired coworkers can all offer assistance. You can also identify and train stay-at-home-mothers who may want a little spending money for a few hours of the day/week to elder-sit your parent(s).

Professionally, there are a whole host of organizations and agencies to help. If long-term care insurance is available, then health and homemaker aides can be service options. Professional agencies deploying visiting home nurses, CNAs, and RNs can help oversee and monitor medical matters. Adult day care facilities are also an option for those that are healthy and independent.

Let's not forget the benefits of today's modern technology. Home-technology advancement, equipment, and remote patient monitoring devices will become your best inner circle of friends. These devices are reliable and dependable, ensure safety, and will ease your peace of mind.

Explore home-security monitoring systems, fall-prevention monitoring systems, home appliances, and cellular phones to take your loved ones' vital signs daily. Soon, in the not-so-distant future, in-home robots will be available to monitor, collect, and send clinical information as well as dispense medications. Human interactions are still the best support system.

8. Need help, ask for help: The life of an unpaid family caregiver is full of emotional swings leading to whirlwind feelings of stress, frustration, guilt, and anger. The first line of defense for breaking up this cycle of emotional

swings is for you to simply ask for help. Also see Dr. Alexis Abramson *"Expert Advise – Avoiding Caregiver Conflict"* [51].

Asking for help starts the restoration and healing process that will allow you to take an emotional respite break to refuel your caregiving energy. Follow these simple steps to help you refuel your passion and peace of mind. Know that family strife and contention will surely come your way.

A) Ask for family help: Engage and solicit help from siblings, relatives, friends, clubs, other agencies, and organizations to help. This begins the process of forming a team, for no one should take on family-caregiving duties and responsibilities alone.

B) Develop a plan and work your plan: Formulating a smart family plan to age-in-place will help family and friends respond quickly and effectively to medical crises when they arise. A carefully crafted family-caregiving plan helps all family members keep focus on the big picture—helping parents.

C) Find support and care for yourself: The circle support system that we previously made a reference to is your caregiving lifeline. Don't hesitate to reach out to professional organizations that have the experience in caring for older people. Do not forget about your own needs. Allow yourself to take a break. Take time to attend to your own needs. Exercise, vacation, sleep, and eating healthy are all good ways to reduce stress.

4) Work and family caregiving - The Reckoning: According to estimates, show some twenty-six to forty-four (26 - 44) million working Americans are caregivers, caring for an aging/disable parent, relative, or friend over fifty ("Caregiving in the US," National Alliance for Caregiving and AARP 2009).

---

51 See more at www.ElderCareResourcesDelaware.com—"Expert Advice: Avoiding Caregiver Conflict"

Employers are becoming more sympathetic to the plight of workers caring for aging love ones. Larger companies have developed new policies and have updated programs to support the family caregivers. Policies like flextime, telecommuting, working from home, and caregiving support groups are now available to aid and assist workers in caring for loved ones.

Special Notice

Who Will Care for You - WWCFY

Community Healthy Aging Training Series (CHATS)
(Website Under Construction)

* * Coming Soon * *

WWCFY - Regional Training Forums
Community Healthy-Aging Training Series (CHATS)

Starting in 2017 there will be scheduled targeted module area workshops addressing: Who Will Care for You...The Reckoning; Living Healthy & Independent; Eating to Live Healthy and other workshop topics. Workshops are part of the Community Healthy Aging Training Series (CHATS) multifaceted educational forum.

Targeted module area workshops are for consumers, of all ages -- Baby-boomers and young adults (ages 30-52). Participants will learn about the coming caregiving "Silver Age" reckoning crisis... And learn about the seven core (7) components to formulate aging-in-place action plans, for a future lifestyle of health & wellness, senior independence, and a safeguarded quality of life!

Workshops are presented in two distinct formats: (1) a two-hour community introductory workshops at various local locations and (2) a comprehensive, sixteen-hour regional workshop at a hotel/conference center or other designated location. Regional workshops are on a limited basis according to conference host or availability and consumer interest.

Scheduling begins in the fall of 2017, and workshops can be scheduled through the project website (currently under construction beginning the spring 2017).

About The Author

John D. Hemphill is a 37-year retired Senior Public Health Advisor from the Centers for Disease Control (CDC) and the U.S. Department of Health and Human Services (DHHS). Before retiring, 2010, he spent his last 10 years at CDC, Division of Injury Response at the National Center for Injury Prevention and Control (NCIPC). There he focused his public health efforts on expanding the capacity for Injury Surveillance in states and promoting Fall Injury Prevention. His passion for Fall Injury Prevention guided him to become an advocate endorsing universal design solutions as an effective fall injury -- environmental home modification intervention for all adults to stay healthy and safe, living in their home (Aging-in-Place).

In addition to his many years working on public health prevention programs he and his wife, spent time serving as unpaid family caregivers for both aging parents. He and his wife, a registered nurse, spent the past 38+ years as distant family caregivers for his aging parents and the past 12 years as full-time in-home family caregivers for his in-laws.

John has parlayed his public health and family caregiving experiences to create key lifestyle principles for living longer, better to maintain independence to age-in-place. In an effort to share his passion for caregiving lessons learned, he has taken the time to publish the first book edition. ***The Reckoning--Who Will Care for You!***

Acknowledgment

The heart and soul of this book truly goes out to all who have made this two and half year endeavor writing this book become a major accomplishment. There are many individuals who have help me accomplish this feat, numerous family, friends and colleagues who have provided support, counsel and direction.

Let me first acknowledge and give a special thanks to my wife Patricia of forty-two years. She was and still is the real caregiver. I was just her helper taking notes to later tell our story. Pat spent almost twelve years of her active adult life taking time to care for her parents in our home. Her tireless efforts, rooted and grounded, in the love and caring for both her parents, patients at work, her children and me will undoubtedly be rewarded when it's our time. I hope that we were instrumental in someway setting an example for our kids and people across the nation to learn from.

Second, I must give special love and consideration to my two daughters, Nicole and Nina, (adults with children of their own). They have given me, along with my grandchildren, (Alannah, Elle and Miles), the necessary gifts to complete this task and to become the best father and pop-pop I could be. Their understanding for missing out on vacation trips and other family engagements were due to our caregiving duties and responsibilities.

My sincere thanks go out to my public health colleagues for their inspiration, leadership, direction and emotional support over the years. Some are gone home now (Ben and Wayne) but they have always given me purpose that will surely not be forgotten. Also, the tireless and seldom unappreciated family caregivers--thank you: Carol Whittington, Valerie McCier, Dana DeCosta who have taken the time to tell their family story. I must apologize for those interviews and caregiver stories not told in this first edition.

A note of thanks goes out to Jared Reeder for the artistic design of the book jacket cover. Thank you Faye McDonald, Deborah Sorgel and Dawn Douglas, for their time and efforts proofreading and the content editing. Thank you as well to my brother and sister, Calvin and Lain, for their comments and encouragements.

Last a special note of thanks to Shaurnette Crawford for her epiphany for the title of the book... Who Will Care for You! Also, thank you to contributing writers Pam Goldstein, and Jerry Stedman. Thank you also to other professional area experts who have guided me along the way. Finally to all, thank you again for helping me share key *living healthy* tools and tips to help you stay active, healthy and independent.

Printed in the United States
By Bookmasters